British-born John George Brown was a well-known portraitist and genre painter of the late nineteenth century. In his New York City studio he painted denizens of the city's streets such as shoeshine boys and ragamuffins as well as members of the social élite. For many years he and his family summered in Vermont, often in the small village of Cuttingsville, where he painted a number of Vermont scenes, some of which hang in the Shelburne Museum. One of his subjects was a local woman, Mrs. Boutwell, who made quilts to sell to visitors staying at the Union House hotel in Cuttingsville. Seen here in her kitchen, Mrs. Boutwell had a small apartment over the horse sheds across from the Union House.

Brown immortalized Mrs. Boutwell in 1902; he died in 1913. For many years his paintings were out of fashion, but in recent years they have appreciated in value and today fetch very high prices at auction. The same cannot be said of Mrs. Boutwell's quilts, for none of her work is known to be extant.

PLAIN AND FANCY

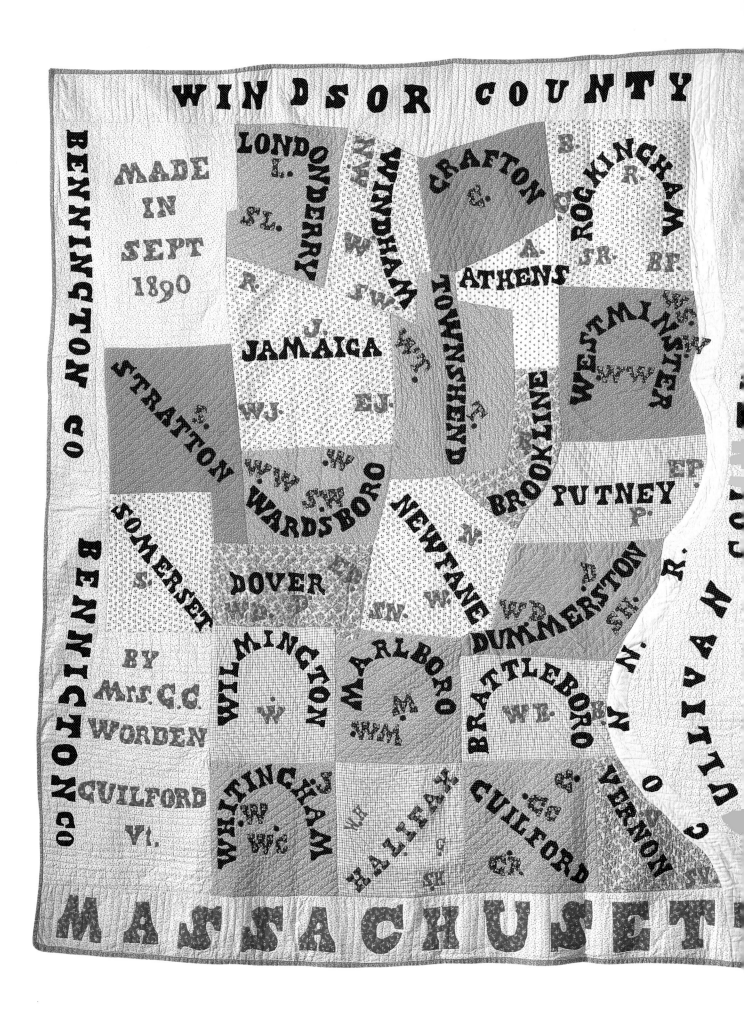

Richard L. Cleveland and Donna Bister

PLAIN

*Vermont's People
And Their Quilts*

AND

*As A Reflection
Of America*

FANCY

THE QUILT DIGEST PRESS

Editorial and production direction by Harold Nadel.
Book and cover design by Kajun Graphics, San Francisco.
Typographical composition by DC Typography, San Francisco.
Printed by Nissha Printing Company, Ltd., Kyoto, Japan.
Color separations by the printer.

Quilt photographs on pages 54 and 59 by Sharon Risedorph, San Francisco.
All other quilt photographs by Ken Burris, Shelburne, Vermont.

First printing.

Library of Congress Cataloging-in-Publication Data

Cleveland, Richard L.
    Plain and fancy: Vermont's people and their quilts as
a reflection of America / Richard L. Cleveland and
Donna Bister.
        p.   cm.
    Includes bibliographical references.
    ISBN 0-913327-30-1 (ppr) : $19.95
    1. Quilts – Vermont – History.   2. Quiltmakers –
Vermont – Biography.   3. Vermont – History.   I. Bister, Donna, 1951– .   II. Title.
NK 9112.C57   1991
746.9'7'09743 – dc20   90-28670
                                                  CIP

The Quilt Digest Press
P.O. Box 1331
Gualala, California 95445

The Quiltsearch Committee gratefully dedicates this book to the owners of the 45 quilts which it describes. Without their trust and cooperation, this project would not have been possible.

Carolyn W. Fernandez, Co-chair
Priscilla D. Hatch, Co-chair
Donna Bister
Richard L. Cleveland

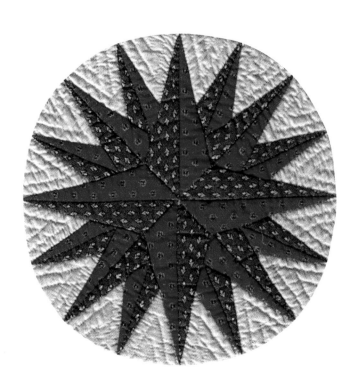

VERMONT QUILTSEARCH
CONTRIBUTORS

The Committee gratefully acknowledges the many gifts in support of our book and touring show. Contributions from the following were received through January 31, 1991.

BUSINESSES AND CORPORATIONS

Union Mutual Fire Insurance Company, Montpelier, VT; Fairfield Processing Corp./Poly-fil,® Danbury, CT; Skydyes (Mickey Lawler), West Hartford, CT; Norton House, Wilmington, VT; Double T Quilt Shop (Pamela Hardiman and Jean Thibodeau), Springfield, MA; House of Sewing & Vacuums, Inc., Essex Junction, VT; Vincent J. Fernandez Oriental Rugs, Richmond, VT; Northfield, VT, businesses: Northfield Savings Bank, Depot Square Pizzeria, Northfield Pharmacy, The Northfield News and Printery, Red Kettle Family Restaurant, Demasi & Ricker, First National Bank of Vermont.

QUILT GUILDS

Vermont guilds: Calico County Quilters, Berlin; Maple Leaf Quilters, Rutland; Champlain Valley Quilters Association, Shelburne; Ox-Bee Quilt Guild, Newbury; Heart of the Land Quilters Guild, Hartland; Fairfax-Georgia Quilters; Quiet Valley Quilter's Guild, Bennington. Out of state: The New England Quilters Guild, Lowell, MA; Eastcoast Quilters' Alliance, Westford, MA; Pine Tree Quilters Guild, ME; Calico Stitchers Quilt Association, Savannah, GA.

INDIVIDUALS AND ORGANIZATIONS

Mary Ann Shepard, Katharine L. Lahee, Robert W. Allen, Joyce Lindner, Barbara S. Wysocki, Jennie McBean, Mary B. Markle, Patsy Orlofsky, Edith E. Diesel, Dorothy Mitchell, Don and Sandra Munsey, Lorrie Sluzenski, Marilyn F. Riley, Evelyn Billings, Bernie and Phyllis Wilcox, Ethel Grandfield, Deborah S. King, Angelika and Granville Brumbaugh, President and Mrs. W. Russell Todd, Mr. and Mrs. James Pedley, Jack and Thelma Baroffio, Edna Zamachaj, Rose Aileen Koretski, An Admiring Calligrapher, Barb and Bill Pope, Anna Spencer, Madeline Hooper, Marya A. Lowe, Joelle King, Mary Jane Dexter, Constance C. Reilly, Cynthia Cano Myers, Marjorie A. Rafuse, Sandy and Lou Schneider, Lynn Leverett Bohi, Pat Morse, Diana Robinson, Karen Fortin, Sara Harter Fredette, Rita Simpson, Louise A. Godbout, Bernice M. Marsh, Lois P. Broder, Joan M. Gasperini, Nancy Brand, Mary E. Reid, Mrs. Lisa E. Card, Monica A. Marcotte, Rozemaryn Van Der Horst, Arthur and Jean Goodrich, Lura Allen Carr, Evelyn Barber, Marjorie J. Dundas, Gladys Grace, Arlene C. Holman, Virginia E. Salter, Margaret LaBarge, Carole and Richard Hinners, Josephine Adams, Deborah M. Beattie, The Ladies Reading Circle (Northfield, VT), Homer and Phoebe Denny, Diana W. Fielder, Gloria Trecartin, Rosemary Pedigo Ponte, Hilda B. Allen, Rochester Vermont Historical Society, Velma W. Wheeler, Louise S. Ripley, Marie Fuller, Sarah Dopp, Dorothy Gilman, Alice and Harry Snyder, Ruth Monte, Constance E. Bastille, Karen I. Siedler Lyons, Avis Spicer, Joanne Anderson, Muriel Walter, Karen Porter, Tonia Sledd, Nola Forbes and her 1990 Fletcher Farm Students, Louise M. Whidden, Daughters of Colonial Wars in the State of Vermont, Donald and Betty Tisdale, Marion Wright, Burney and Florence Taylor, Dr. and Mrs. William H. Feaster, Donald B. Johnstone, Bonnie Knott, Allison Hatch, The Fund for Vermont's Third Century; Faith Tiberio in memory of Michael W. Berry; and five anonymous contributors.

ACKNOWLEDGMENTS

The Committee gratefully acknowledges the assistance of the following in the quilt documentation project and the preparation of this book:

Members of the Vermont Quilt Festival Board of Trustees (Helen Ballard, Joanne Claussen, Carolyn Fernandez, Sarah Knight, Joan Martin, Alice McClaughry, Mary Klett Ryan, Jan Snelling and Betty Tisdale) for their individual and collective support of the project at all stages;

Karey Patterson Bresenhan, for her professional and invaluable training of the documentation staff;

Festival Treasurer Betty Tisdale for keeping track of the finances, Joyce Lindner, Katharine Lahee, Francis C. Leonard, Rosina A. Hanson, Virginia Gunn, Stanley Hatch, Vivian Bryan, Elene Brigham Sartell, Roger and Diana LeClair, Richard and Phyllis Higgins, Burney and Florence Taylor, Northfield News and Printery, Historic Deerfield Inc., and The Vermont Statehood Bicentennial Commission;

For organizing and supervising publicity for the quilt documentation days, Jan Snelling and Mary Klett Ryan, and to people who assisted with those and other mailings in Rutland and in Northfield; and to many Vermont organizations for providing copies of their mailing lists or publicity in their newsletters;

Documentation site assistance: Sites Registrar Pauline Hurley; Joan Martin, Alice McClaughry, Mary Klett Ryan and Jan Snelling; local co-ordinators (Yvonne Isabelle, Jane Reynolds, Louise Ripley, Kathy Frechette, Sylvia Reynolds, Beeda Bailey, Irene Falby, Elizabeth Odell, Nola Forbes, Frances Bouffard, Maureen Lavalette, Kathy Beauregard, Marion Wright, Charlotte Croft, Cyndy Gates, Kate Townsend, Barbara Kennedy, Patricia Wiley, Shirley Twitchell, Aileen Chutter, Ginny Salter, and Sidney and Hildy Lawrence); overnight accommodations (Bessie M. Cleveland, Louise Ripley, Nancy Brown and Alice McClaughry); and over 125 volunteers who worked at the documentation sites;

Staff members at Vermont museums: The Bennington Museum (Ruth Levin, Registrar), The Shelburne Museum (Eloise Beil, Director of Collections; Celia Y. Oliver, Curator; and Pauline Mitchell, Registrar), and The Vermont Historical Society (Jacqueline Calder, Curator; Mary Labate Rogstad, Registrar; Mary Pat Brigham, Library Assistant);

Manuscript readers: Nancy Halpern, Dr. H. N. Muller III, Celia Y. Oliver, Andrew Nemethy, Dr. Ellen Madison, Thomas C. Ryan, Jane E. Bryant; and Robert W. Allen, who typed the original manuscript and captions and all subsequent revisions into computer files and helped edit the text;

For their interest and support, all of the quiltmakers and other friends whose individual contributions had a significant collective impact on the overall project.

Special thanks to Carolyn Wakefield Fernandez and Priscilla Dole Hatch, who co-chaired the Vermont Quiltsearch, for their active participation in the selection of the quilts for this book; for their expertise in evaluating all 1,100 quilts documented during the search; for screening the records of another 2,000 quilts already in the Vermont Quilt Festival files; for further evaluating, collecting and transporting for photography the quilts presented here; and for managing the myriad details of this lengthy and complicated project.

PLAIN AND FANCY

Mariner's Compass, *by Mary Canfield Benedict Baker, Arlington, c. 1850, 90 x 94 inches, pieced and appliquéd cottons.*
Collection of The Shelburne Museum. #3239.

URING THE HALF-CEN-
tury preceding the
American Revolution,
there was enough
going on in what was
becoming the United
States of America to
occupy several genera-
tions of nation builders. From the first
murmurings of dissatisfaction with
England to the Peace of Paris in 1783,
leaders from the thirteen colonies
were kept busy establishing the need
for a war, running the war, and finally
bringing it to a successful close.

On the home front, the mothers, sisters, wives and daughters of these war-
makers and patriots did plenty of
nation-building of their own. They
raised families, tended crops, spun and
wove cloth. From that cloth they made
the family's clothing, as well as its
linens, blankets and quilts. In most of
America, especially in areas where
cash and manufactured goods were in

did the colonies survive and grow.
When war came, they did what women
have always done at such times: they
worked, prayed, raised children,
buried their dead, wept and went on
with their lives.

At war's end, independence was won
but commerce was wounded. American trade with Britain was severely
curtailed; imports and exports both
suffered, as Americans were thrown
onto their own resources. American
ingenuity (which New Englanders are
pleased to call "Yankee ingenuity")
was about to come into its own.

Vermont was the frontier of New
England, the wild, ragged edge of civi-
lization, long after the other states of
the region were settled. By 1640,
twenty years after the landing at Plymouth, permanent English colonies
existed at Boston, Hartford, Provi-
dence, Portsmouth and Portland; not
until 1724, nearly a century later, was
the first permanent European settle-

The end of the French and Indian
Wars brought security to western New
England. The resulting growth of
established cities and towns pushed
some people, disaffected and restless,
to seek opportunities elsewhere. Land
in the New Hampshire Grants, as Vermont was called then, was plentiful
and relatively cheap, so it was north-
ward, ho, for thousands of Connecticut and Massachusetts folk. In 1760,
Vermont's estimated population was
300; by 1791, it had skyrocketed to
85,425.[2]

Problems were created by confusion
as to which of His Britannic Majesty's
colonies had the right to grant land in
the territory between the Connecticut
River and Lake Champlain. New York
and New Hampshire both claimed
those 9,600 square miles; the dispute
raged for decades, and the crown
finally decided in New York's favor.
But the royal decision failed to end the
dispute. In many of the 128 towns
granted by New Hampshire, settlers
who purchased their land in good faith
were informed by New York authorities that they held invalid titles, and
that they would have to repurchase the
properties.

The direct result of these disputes
was the organization in the summer of
1770 of the Green Mountain Boys.
Commanded by that ructious man,
Ethan Allen, this informal militia
defended the residents of the New
Hampshire Grants against the claims
and courts of the New Yorkers. The
group was also useful when hostilities
finally broke out with Great Britain,
providing an armed and partially-
trained fighting force in several battles
of the American Revolution. Ethan
Allen and his brothers were no knights
on white horses; their involvement on
behalf of the Vermonters contained a
large measure of enlightened self-
interest. Ethan and Ira Allen and
others of their brothers and associates
bought and sold thousands of acres of
land in Vermont. They made and lost
fortunes, and made — but rarely lost —
enemies.

In Vermont, which came through
the Revolution without the huge debts
which weighed down many other
states, the Governor, Council and

◁ *Here is a quilt with an impeccable Vermont pedigree. It is said to have been
made by Mary Canfield Benedict prior to her marriage to Fayette Sheppard
Baker in 1852. The Canfields and the Bakers were among the earliest settlers of
Arlington. The Bakers had an early sheep-shearing and wool-carding industry
on the Battenkill River in Arlington. Fayette was related to Remember Baker,
cousin of Ethan Allen and one of the original Green Mountain Boys.*

The Mariner's Compass, *with its thirty-two long, sharply-pointed pieces,
needs the touch of an advanced quiltmaker. Even the sashing in this striking
quilt is complex, the mark of a woman for whom geometry held no terrors.
Depending upon the maker's skill, the middle of the compass may look like
Mary Benedict Baker's, or it may have a circle appliquéd over it to hide the fact
that the points do not meet precisely. That a woman of not quite twenty years
had the skill to complete such a quilt should not surprise us, since most girls
began sewing as early as five or six years of age.*

*When they married in 1852, Fayette was twenty-two and Mary was twenty.
They operated a farm for many years. Fayette died in 1900 at the age of seventy;
Mary died in 1920, one month short of her ninetieth birthday.*

*The author Dorothy Canfield Fisher, a later member of that Arlington family,
signed her own name to another Bennington County quilt nearly a century later
(see page 92).*

short supply, such activity was necessary and constant. In pioneer communities and in isolated homes far from
those settlements, America's women
were its manufacturers; most of what
was consumed in the home had to be
prepared there, and it was up to the
women to see that the job got done. On
their backs and by their labors, as
surely as upon those of their menfolk,

ment established in Vermont.[1]

The woods and rivers of Vermont
provided a guerrilla freeway between
Canada and New England through the
seventeenth and eighteenth centuries.
The French and British, and their
respective Indian allies, cruised back
and forth, each administering dreadful
atrocities upon the other's settlements
at either end of Vermont.

General Assembly presided over a self-declared independent nation, the Republic of Vermont. From its declaration of independence on January 15, 1777,[3] Vermont went its own way. Rebuffed by the Continental Congress in its repeated requests for recognition as a state, principally on the objection of New York, Vermont maintained its independence for fourteen years.

In the years from independence to statehood, the population grew rapidly, the people spreading themselves across the state from south to north and following the valleys and the Crown Point Military Road. Like pioneers throughout history, they were, by and large, a hardy and resourceful lot. They brought what possessions they could from their former homes, but to a large extent they had to start with little. With the end of the Revolution, residents no longer had to worry about attacks by the British or their Indian allies. There were plenty of other hazards, though; accidents, hardships and disease carried many to early deaths, but still the people persisted, and Vermont prospered and grew.

Towns expanded to accommodate the needs of farmers, and trade within and without the Republic thrived. The great inland waterway, Lake Champlain, carried Vermont goods north to Canada, an orientation which continued until the Champlain Canal connected the lake to the Hudson River. Wheat fields covered much of the fertile Champlain Valley, and for a short time Vermont exported grain to the new nation.

Once farms were established, Vermont's economy, like that of the rest of the United States, was sustained by more than agriculture. Numerous small industries dotted the countryside. Forges, window sash and blind factories, sawmills, potteries, leather-tanning operations, chair-manufacturing concerns and even breweries could be found across the state.

The earliest cash crop, however, came from the manufacture and export of potash, not just in Vermont but in colonial and early post-Revolutionary America generally. Potash was an ingredient of the soap of the time and, as such, was vital in the washing

process for the manufacture of woolen goods. The demand in Britain was enormous; in 1767, it was estimated that England and Ireland alone imported over 3,000 tons. Potash was so valuable that it often fetched ten times the price of a comparable amount of wheat. Many Vermont farms had a potash kettle, because the raw material was there—the trees they cut to clear the land. Burning these and boiling the ashes produced the potash which would have been the sole income for many early families.

America's first patent was for an improved method of making potash, issued to Vermonter Samuel Hopkins in 1791. By that year, over 1,000 tons of potash were being exported annually from Vermont. Most American potash was shipped to Europe, and its value was enormous, but, as European sources were developed, American exports fell. By about 1814, potash exports dropped to zero, and it ceased being an economic factor in Vermont.[4] Vermont's potash prosperity was soon eclipsed by a cash crop which went about on four legs.

Richardson sawmill in Stockbridge (see page 56). Courtesy of Mary Ordway Davis.

"ALL WOOL AND A yard wide" is an old New England saying denoting quality. It dates from a time when the material you purchased might *not* be all wool, and would almost certainly have been less than 36" wide (at least until wider looms were built). It is also a reminder of the important place sheep held in Vermont life for many decades.

America's earliest European settlers were farmers before they were anything else. To their designated plot of land they would bring whatever clothing and furnishings their oxen could pull in carts, or they themselves could carry on sledges or their backs. They might also have a milking cow, possibly a pig, and probably one or two sheep. As important as pigs and cattle were, the sheep became almost more important, for it was a renewable resource: its back would provide wool for clothing and bedding, year after year. With cows and pigs, once you'd eaten the meat and used the skin, that was the end.

Sheep were a staple of New England life for decades. The wool quilts so common to the region came in part from wool from these sheep. The batting might have been made from odd bits left from the shearing, and the backing, which tends to be coarser than the tops, might have been made on or near the family farm. The tops, on the other hand, at least after cash became more plentiful, were far more likely to have been made of fabrics imported from England, even into the 1830's.

The two wool quilts in this book provide very different examples of the work of these early quiltmakers. The pieced Rich quilt, c. 1780-1800, (page 32) contains both wool and linen, most of which had been used previously, but its pink fabric is almost certainly imported. The whole-cloth Stoddard quilt (page 18), dated 1826, is more characteristic of Vermont wool quilts. The olive top and orange back are in strips ranging from 25½" to 29¾" wide, and the back is slightly coarser

Consul William Jarvis was about eighty-five years old when this lithograph was made. His introduction of Merino sheep into Vermont and their impact upon the state and its people during the nineteenth century can hardly be overstated.

There is a wool coverlet made in Danby, Vermont, in March 1821, by a woman who identified herself only by the initials E. K. This coverlet, in the collection of the Woodstock (Vermont) Historical Society, consists of many narrow strips of various designs, including animals, fish and buildings, as well as a multitude of geometric patterns.

Made just a decade after the Merinos were brought to Vermont, the coverlet has a verse woven into it which emphasizes the importance of the sheep:

> *The vallies smile with bending corn*
> *White flocks the verdant hills adorn*
> *The voice of plenty cheers the morn*
> *Thrice happy land America.*

> *Columbia lives by arts of peace*
> *As agricultures fruits increase*
> *Her noble flocks of finest fleece*
> *Bid manufactures flourish here.*

Courtesy of Weathersfield Historical Society.

than the top. The top might have been of imported fabric, though it is not glazed.

Midway between the Rich and Stod-

dard quilts, a revolution began in Vermont, caused by a young man from Boston named William Jarvis. Appointed American consul to Lisbon in 1801 by President Jefferson,[5] Jarvis took an interest in the huge flocks of Merino sheep he saw in the Portuguese and Spanish countryside. Their wool was finer and heavier than that of the American breeds, but exportation was strictly forbidden by the crown. Shortly after 1800, David Humphreys, American consul in Madrid, shipped 200 of the prized ovines to the U. S., but President Jefferson's trade embargo put a halt to such trade. Several years later, Jarvis acquired as many as 4,000 altogether, though estimates vary, and sent them off to America. Most he sold in New York and Massachusetts at high prices, but in 1811 he brought some 400 to his newly acquired property in Weathersfield, Vermont.[6]

Once here, the Merinos thrived; they took over the Vermont countryside, and their fine reputation led to the exportation of many across the United States and around the world. In later years, many Australian and New Zealand flocks got their start from Merinos shipped from Vermont. The growth of the flocks in Vermont was phenomenal. Through cycles of changing demand, sheep-raising reached its peak in Vermont by about 1840, bringing prosperity to many hill farms. If in the South cotton was king, in Vermont the sheep became emperor; Vermont became a one-crop state, where sheep outnumbered humans by seven to one.[7] (By contrast, the cows who for so long outnumbered the people here did so by a margin of only about eight to seven.[8])

Vermont sheep farmers were aided by the federal tariffs of the 1820's. The removal of those duties by the late 1840's and competition from huge Western flocks signaled an end to the period of Vermont's greatest prosperity, and by the end of the decade the flocks began to decline sharply. Not even the Civil War, with its demand for wool uniforms, could salvage what had been Vermont's greatest industry; by the 1870's, the era of the Merino was finished.[9]

With its olive green top and pale orange back (possibly dyed with jewelweed), this elaborately-quilted piece of work was destined for Lucia Stoddard's hope chest (although six years elapsed between securing the last stitch of the quilt and the tying of the knot between Lucia and Seth Walker). She was proud enough of her work (perhaps not a very New England attitude for one descended from so many Congregational preachers) to quilt her initials, age and year of her birth into this quilt.

New England's, and Vermont's, wool quilts were a varied lot. Anyone who has seen any of these in museum collections knows that they are a riot of colors; virtually any color which could be produced in a dye might find its way into wool for a quilt. Unlike many of its contemporaries, the Stoddard quilt was not glazed.

Whole Cloth, by Lucia Stoddard Walker, Waitsfield, 1826, 88 x 86 inches, wool.
Collection of the Randolph Historical Society, Inc. #2164.

For all its simplicity, this quilt is an original concept, the sort of creation which might cause another quiltmaker to smite her brow and exclaim, "Why didn't I think of that!" Muted though its colors are now, this quilt once was brighter. The stripes which now read as browns and tans were purples and lavenders, their fading the result of unstable dyes. The quilting is fine and heavy, boxes within boxes covering most of the surface. A delicate vine-and-leaf motif swirls through the diagonal muslin strips.

Though the name of the maker is unknown, it is presumed to have been one of the women of the Ballard family, early settlers of Georgia, Vermont.

LeMoyne Star *with diagonal stripes, unknown maker, probably Georgia, c. 1850–1870, 86 x 88½ inches, pieced cottons.*
Collection of Alden and Rebecca Ballard. #2345.

I N THE HALF-CENTURY FROM THE election of Thomas Jefferson in 1800 to the deaths of John C. Calhoun, Henry Clay and Daniel Webster between 1850 and 1852, almost everything about America changed. The physical boundaries were radically different; much of the midwest was settled, Texas entered the union and, on the Pacific Ocean, the former California Republic now anchored the nation in the west. Much of the Whig program of national improvements had come to pass (but by state and private, not federal, doing); canals, roads and even the first railroads began to reach across the country, connecting east to west, north to south. These improvements meant new markets for some farmers and manufacturers, disaster for others.

Another war with the mother country came in 1812 and lasted until 1814. It was the last time Britain and the United States warred; though points of contention cropped up for several more decades, sometimes fueled by politicians in each country who saw advantage to be gained from beating on the other, it was left to diplomats rather than generals to sort out the differences. Instead of the British, the U.S. had the Mexicans and the Indians to beat up, and many Americans found this more satisfying than fighting their trans-Atlantic cousins.

Politically, the torch passed from the generation of the revolution-makers to men who knew of the war of liberty only from the stories of their fathers and grandfathers. The years from 1820 to 1850 were dominated by three men from different sections of the nation: Calhoun of South Carolina, Clay of Kentucky and Webster of Massachusetts. Slavery increasingly became the litmus test by which other national questions were judged. Abolitionism, scorned at first as the rantings of radicals, grew in adherents in the north and led indirectly to the demise of the Whigs and to the creation of the anti-slavery Republican Party.

In art and literature, Americans began to make themselves known in Europe, while American science built upon Europe's industrial revolution, improving as it went, creating a power-

△ *Even after the great sheep-raising days had passed, a few farmers maintained small flocks, such as this one on the Ballard Farm, where the quilt on page 19 was made. As the flocks dwindled, pastures as rocky and barren as the one pictured here grew up to brush and then back to forest. William Ballard is shown here between 1935 and 1940.*

ful manufacturing base. Thousands of European immigrants poured into this country, bringing their own traditions to mix with those of the predominantly Anglo-Saxon population. Native and newcomer alike headed west, always expanding the frontier, always pushing the limits of settlement, always looking for grass which,

if it wasn't greener, was more plentiful—and cheaper. Once there, they sliced into the dense, rich midwestern soil with steel plows made in Illinois by the Vermont-born blacksmith John Deere.

In Vermont, the half-century was one of rising, and then declining, social, cultural and political turmoil. At times Vermont seemed to be two different states: the east side was more conservative in politics and religion, a bastion of Connecticut Congregationalism. West of the dividing mountains, radicalism was more prevalent; when there *was* religion, it was a more energetic variety of Protestantism than in the east. Mormonism had its birth here (literally—Joseph Smith, Brigham Young and Oliver Cowdery among others were born in Vermont),

*Photographed by W. D. Chandler (negative number ATX 575). From
Vermont Album – A Collection of Early Vermont Photographs, ed. Ralph Nading Hill,
Copyright ©1974 by The Stephen Greene Press. Used by permission.*

though it had to go west to prosper.

Besides the religious activity, there were social experiments. In Putney, John Humphrey Noyes assembled his family and some friends into a commune of sorts, sharing all property. This was fine as far as it went, but when they started sharing spouses, then the authorities resolved to put an end to it. Noyes and his followers decamped from Putney barely ahead of the Windham County sheriff (so the legend says) and ended up in Oneida, New York, where their community flourished and made a grand name for itself and its products. Noyes wasn't the only social tinkerer; there were movements of every description, home-grown and imported, each catering, however briefly, to some segment of the population which found their

theologies or philosophies appealing. Those who didn't like the existing Isms could start their own sect, and often did.

From 1800 until 1850, the population continued to grow; for a time Vermont sent six representatives to the U.S. House, compared with six for Tennessee, five for Ohio and six for New Jersey. Today Vermont has one U.S. Representative; the others have nine, twenty-one and fourteen respectively. Politically, the state passed from the control of the men who made the Republic and who tended toward Jeffersonianism to a younger, some-

what more conservative generation. In politics, as in social and religious movements, the orthodox and the unorthodox existed side by side, but not always easily.

Temperance and abolitionism made inroads in the state, though residents were by no means unanimous on either subject. Sooner or later, most of the movements which swept the rest of the nation arrived in Vermont. It was a period of profound ferment which was slowed and then stopped only by the coming of the Civil War and the continued exodus of Vermonters to other parts of the United States.

Family tradition says that Sarah Ann Dewey made this quilt just before her marriage to Reuben Clapp Allen in 1841, with the help of Reuben's sisters Lucretia and Celinda. Her quilt is a romantic floral fantasy; even the narrow binding is stenciled with a matching pattern of flowers and feathers.

Stenciled quilts are quite rare, and one wonders where Sarah Ann got the idea to make one. Perhaps she, or her future sisters-in-law, had seen something similar and decided to try it themselves. The Allen sisters were related to the Allens of Deerfield and Ashfield, Massachusetts, and there is a similar quilt in the collection of Historic Deerfield.*

Sarah Ann and Reuben married in March of 1841, settling in North Hero near Reuben's family. Five years later, Sarah was dead, leaving her husband, two small children, and a lovely quilt still treasured by her descendants.

*Correspondence from owner, dated October 23, 1989.

Floral Stencil, by Sarah Ann Dewey Allen, North Hero, c. 1841, 90 x 90 inches, cottons.
Private collection, Vermont. #292.

Here is a classic pattern, the familiar North Carolina Lily (known by various names in various parts of the country), but with a difference. The usual color combination was green with red or pink (sometimes both), but this one is unabashedly yellow. Perhaps in it the maker tried to replicate yellow daylilies which grew in the yard of her farm. If that was her inspiration, then this quilt must have provided a cheerful — and much-needed — wintertime reminder of Vermont's all-too-brief spring and summer.

The family quilts descended to daughters; all of Electa's quilts have come to her great-granddaughter. (The owner has also several made by Alice Ann Warner, Electa's daughter, who had the requisite thirteen when she married. Unlike her mother, Alice Ann numbered each of her quilts in ink.)

North Carolina Lily, by Electa Thankful Barnes Warner, Pittsford, c. 1850–1870, 88 x 72 inches, pieced cottons.
Collection of Katharine E. Dopp. #159.

A QUAKER FAMILY

THIS WONDERFUL *OAK LEAF* APPLIQUÉ, THOUGHT TO have been made by a woman of the Hoag family, was called the "Quaker quilt" by its later owners. The Hoags were members of the Society of Friends, along with many other early settlers of the west side of the island of Grand Isle. Well before 1800, the Hoags and other Grand Isle Quakers made their way into the Lake Champlain islands from settlements in New York's Dutchess County, whence they had come even earlier from Connecticut. From the islands they spread to other Vermont communities, several of which had sizeable Quaker populations well into the mid-nineteenth century.

Daniel and Phebe Mosher Hoag built their log cabin in the spring of 1788, adjacent to land on which the Quaker meeting house was constructed in 1827. About 1793, when the farm was thriving, the family replaced the log cabin with a frame house which still stands, occupied today by one of their direct descendants. About 1840, one of Daniel and Phebe's fourteen children, James, married his cousin Amy, one of ten children born to Edward and Mercy Briggs Hoag. To James and Amy were born eight children.

After Daniel Hoag's death in 1809, his estate was valued at $3,045.09. His barn and outbuildings were filled with turkeys, oxen, milk and beef cattle, horses and sheep. Oats, buckwheat, hay and hemp filled the lofts and storage bins. Like the inventory of the Rich estate (see page 33), every item was listed. Included were four bed quilts, "part worn," with a value of $8.50, one bed quilt "part made" worth $1.50, and two more bed quilts already in the possession of his daughters, valued at $2.00 and $4.50.

At various times, the Hoags raised flax and hemp, shipped apples and made cider (the cider press still stands) and produced maple sugar. They also raised sheep; like most Vermont farmers, they switched to dairy cows when the value of wool declined. Evidence of this transition can be seen in the barn, which was jacked up to make room for the cattle. In 1803 and again in the 1860's, the house was remodeled; in 1915, running water was added, and in 1938 the farm was electrified. It continued to be a working farm into the 1970's. A collection of books, including legal and educational texts as well as favorite classics, attests to the fact that the family was well-read and had a lively interest in the world.

The Hoags remained active in the local Quaker society until it disbanded about 1860. Quakers were in the forefront of many social movements in the last century, including abolitionism, temperance and women's rights. James Hoag, Daniel's son, acted upon the society's principles of pacifism by refusing to report for militia duty. He was taken in a wagon, seated in his own chair, to the county courthouse for punishment. Since he refused to change his mind, the court told James he could go home. He said, "Thee hast brought me here, thee canst take me back," which they did.

Today, Quakers in Vermont number fewer adherents than in the nineteenth century, but the lovely Hoag quilt continues to remind us of their gentle presence.

▷ *The* Oak Leaf *was a popular appliqué pattern of the last century. This one is unusual because it is done solely in green and uses a garden maze setting to separate the blocks.*

Quakers were known as "plain" people for their simple style of dress and avoidance of elaborate social and religious rituals. The "Quaker" quilt, as it was called by later generations, is neither plain nor simple. It speaks of skill, patience and persistence, and a love of color and design.

Oak Leaf, *by a member of the Hoag family, Grand Isle, c. 1850–1870, 86 x 88 inches, pieced and appliquéd cottons. Private collection, Vermont. #2835.*

Photographed by Frank Crozier, c. 1908 (negative number ATX 652). From
Vermont Album – A Collection of Early Vermont Photographs, *ed. Ralph Nading Hill,*
Copyright ©1974 by The Stephen Greene Press. Used by permission.

Whitingham Academy, built in 1842, stood abandoned thirty years later as changing patterns of population reduced the student body below the number needed to keep the school open. By the time this photograph was made, the settlement of Whitingham Center was no longer even a small village as people chose to live and do business in other nearby communities.

"BLEST BE THE TIE THAT binds" is the first line of an old hymn, but in this context it refers to the signature, friendship or autograph quilts which so often served as tokens of love and esteem among friends. It also serves as a reminder of the migration of Americans during the nineteenth century.

Unlike Europeans, from whom most Americans were descended, the population of the New World seemed always to be on the move. Even in the earliest colonial times, people pulled up roots and moved to all points of the compass. They were ever restless, ever in search of better opportunities or more land. In 1850 the census determined that one-third of Americans lived outside the state or nation in which they were born.[10] Opening of new lands and improvements in transportation accelerated this process. This was true in Vermont, too, but while many sons and daughters left, out-migration was not the only story; even in the decades which showed a net loss in population, there were always new people moving in.

Almost as quickly as the population of Vermont rose, due mostly to settlers eager for land in the Green Mountains, parts of it began to move away. Before 1820, Vermonters began packing up, selling out, moving on, driven away partly by the frightful weather of 1816 – a judgment, some said, from God. "The year of no summer" it was called; even 150 years later, Vermonters still referred to it as "Eighteen Hundred and Froze to Death."[11] Snow fell or a frost occurred every month of the year, crops failed and livestock died; it was a period of great hardship, and it pushed many wavering Vermonters over the edge and out of state.

By the thousands they headed for Ohio, Indiana and Illinois; wherever restless Americans went, there were the Vermonters. When there were neither trains nor boats, they rode in wagons, and when there were no wagons, they rode on horseback, and when there were no horses, as was fre-

quently the case, they walked. They were Vermonters, bred of the stony hills to lives without luxury, born of the pioneers and ready to be pioneers again. They took with them their learning, their desire to get ahead, their inventiveness and persistence.

Often their letters home were filled with longing, but mainly for the friends and family left behind, not for the lives which late they led. It was in these homesick times, especially for the women, who usually had no say in the move, that the friendship quilts played an important part.

The craze for friendship quilts began in the early 1840's and lasted until the 1870's.[12] It began on the Eastern seacoast and gradually spread west with America's mobile population. Signing linens and quilts has a long history in this country, but names or initials were usually rendered in cross-stitch or running stitch because inks were unstable and tended to eat through fabrics. The introduction of improved inks allowed women to sign their quilts and linens with a pen without the fear of damage. The craze was probably given further impetus by the interest in autograph albums which began in the preceding decade.

Unlike the appliqué album, or sampler, quilts which appeared at about the same time and which often bore signatures as well, the friendship quilt didn't necessarily require the purchase of numerous fabrics. Because it was usually a scrap quilt of small pieces, it could be made from remnants from any woman's scrap basket. Unlike the bulky autograph albums, the individual quilt blocks could easily be sent through the mail, so signatures could be obtained from people who lived at a distance.

As a rule, quilts made prior to the mid-1850's were more elaborate in their inscriptions, often based on the flowery examples found in popular magazines. After the middle 1850's, inscriptions generally were shorter, often consisting only of the signer's name. Thousands and thousands of friendship quilts were made from the 1840's to the 1870's, and so great was

their popularity that a woman might have had her name on more than one during her lifetime.[13]

Six of the quilts in this book bear signatures, and in most cases the signatures are rendered in ink by the presumed signer, but there the resemblance ends. They span a full century, from 1850 to 1950, and are rendered in six different patterns. Three are from the period of the friendship quilt's greatest popularity, the 1840's and 1850's.[14] Of these three, two appear to have been made for people who moved away, one from Connecticut to Vermont and the other from Randolph, Vermont, to an unknown destination. The third, whose purpose is unknown, bears 143 names and the date 1853.

Of the other three, the *Hole in the Barn Door* (page 31) was a fund-raising device and the *Nine Patch* variation (page 45) was a roster of friends, family and maple-sugar customers, many of whom lived in the midwest, reminders of that great wave of migration. The sixth was really a guest book for its owner, and its story will be told later on.

Sarah Smith's friends and family from Massachusetts and Connecticut sent the album quilt (page 63) to be with her in West Rochester, Vermont, on the hill farm her husband began clearing in 1838. Most blocks are simply signed in spidery script, but one contains the words "New London, Willimantic and Palmer Railroad." Another quotes from the Bible, saying "thy father's friend, forsake not." All of the dates are from 1850.

The hexagon quilt (page 29) is more of a curiosity. Bearing all of those names and the one date of 1853, it carries no clue as to its origins. Would that its signers had been as forthcoming as those on some of the other friendship quilts of the period. Whatever its intended purpose, it was obviously dear to the young woman who possessed it for, like so many others of its type, it was carefully put away and lovingly handed down from one generation to the next. The friendship quilts were a tangible reminder to the recipients that they were loved and missed.

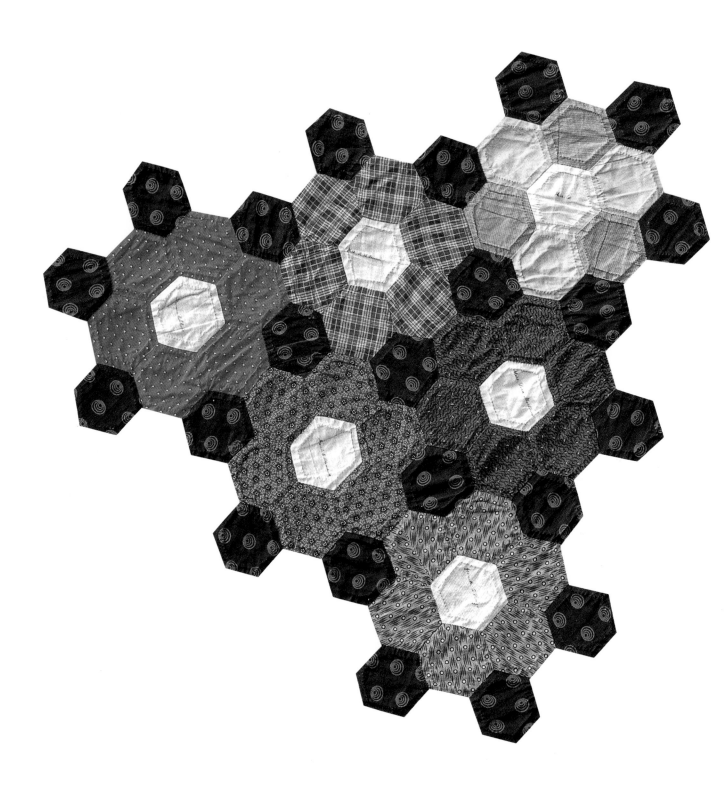

We don't know for certain that Mary Flint made this quilt. Her name is on it, along with 142 others. It seems unlikely that it would have been made for her wedding; Mary Flint wed Edgar Hatch six years later, in 1859. Perhaps it was a charity fund-raiser, each person making a small contribution to have her name written on a block and to have a chance at keeping the quilt for her own.

As is too often the case, the history of this piece has been lost. It was found with several other quilts in a trunk at the family farm in Central Vermont, after the death of the last family members who might remember the story.

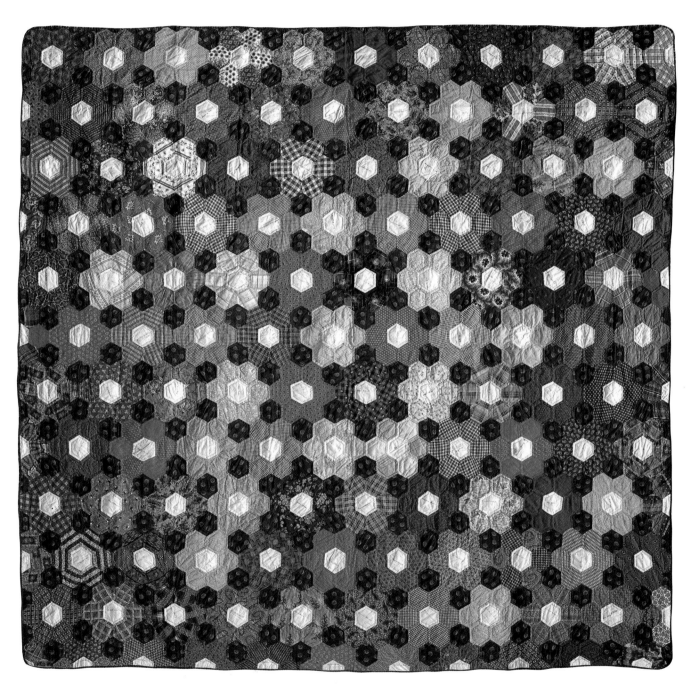

Hexagon, possibly by Mary Flint Hatch, West Randolph, 1853, 82 x 85 inches, pieced cottons.
Collection of Jim and Clara Abbott. #2196.

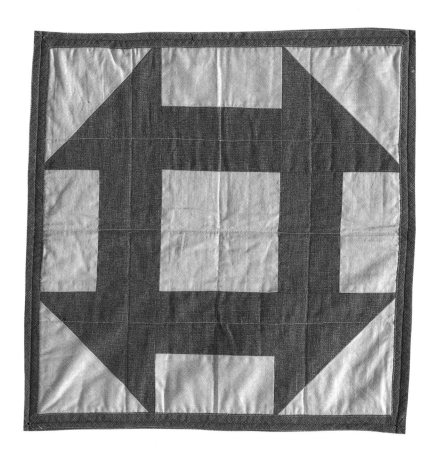

At first glance, this appears to be a strictly utilitarian quilt. When you turn it over, there on the back are 774 names, most of the people who lived in West Concord, Vermont, in 1895. Someone wrote the number in the center block with another piece of important information: "Pieced by the Y.P.C.U. of West Concord, Vt. Spring of 1895." According to the Concord Historical Society (current owner of the piece), the Y.P.C.U. was the Young People's Christian Union, a youth group affiliated with the Universalist Church.

The Society speculates that the quilt was made to raise money for some project or activity of the Y.P.C.U., each name representing a small cash contribution. Whatever the project was, it must have been a very popular one, for the names listed represent most of the town. Many of the names are still familiar in Concord (West Concord changed its name to Concord in 1904) and the Y.P.C.U.'s simple quilt is a wonderful historical document.

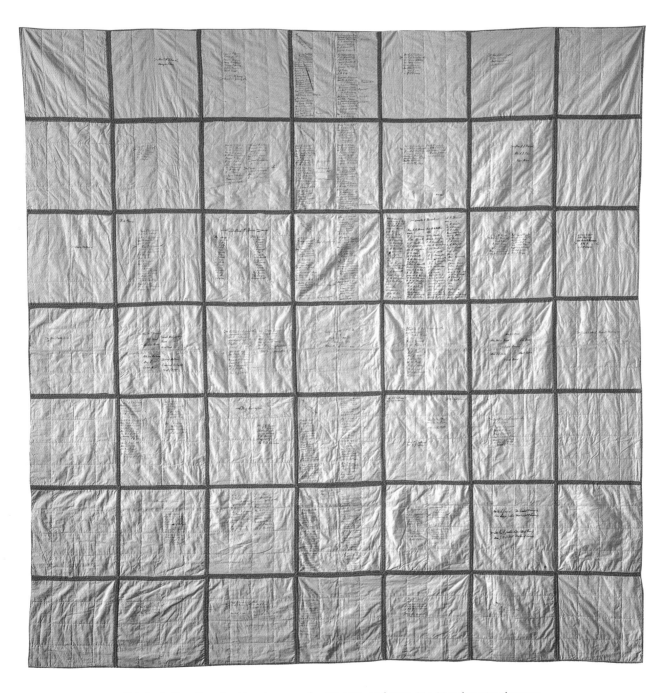

Hole in the Barn Door *(back), unknown maker, West Concord, 1895, 86 x 86 inches, pieced cottons.*
Collection of Concord Historical Society, Inc. #3019.

Nine Patch *variation, probably by Catherine Sophia Whiteman Rich, Maidstone, c. 1780–1800, 90 x 88 inches, pieced wools and linens. Collection of Georgina Greene Hurd and Mary Greene Lighthall. #2960.*

TWO PIONEERS

JOHN AND CATHERINE SOPHIA RICH WERE AMONG THE early settlers of Vermont. They and their families were uprooted not from the British Isles but from the European continent. Both were born in Germany, he in 1729 and she in 1738. Like many who followed, once they arrived in America their names were changed to accommodate American tongues: his Reich became Rich, and her Weydman became Whiteman.

With other German Protestants and French Huguenots, they were brought to Massachusetts in 1751, to a colony hungry for skilled artisans. In 1753 John and Catherine were married and took up residence in western Massachusetts. By 1778 they had moved northeast, to Haverhill, New Hampshire, in the upper Connecticut River valley. Their third and last move took them sixty miles up the Connecticut River, to Maidstone, Vermont, in 1784, just a year after the peace treaty was signed by the new United States and Great Britain.

Their German birth was no bar to their acceptance; between 1785 and 1790, Maidstone's voters elected John five times to represent them in Vermont's General Assembly. It was in January, 1791, during his last term, that John Rich and 104 of his colleagues voted to ratify the Constitution of the United States of America. By their act, they ended nearly fourteen years of independence and brought Vermont into the union of states.

By hard work, the family prospered in Maidstone. When John died September 30, 1813, he left an estate of $3,922.72, a very large sum in those days. The inventory of the estate lists everything he owned, even to the individual knives, pots and kettles.

Among the items listed are: 40 yards of woolen cloth, 19 yards of fulled cloth (partly processed wool), 12 yards of undifferentiated cloth, "Sundry remnants of Cloth," and 172 yards of "linnen & cotten & linen Cloth." The value of this cloth, which totaled over 243 yards, was

◁ *This* Nine Patch *variation is an excellent example of an early pieced quilt. Pieced wool quilts made prior to 1800 are not unknown in New England; they exist in museums and private collections and in quilt reference books. Still, in Vermont whole cloth was the rule, pieced the exception, among wool quilts.*

The quilt has seen considerable use since it was made at the end of the eighteenth century, probably by Catherine Sophia Whiteman Rich. It was not hard use, though, which accounted for the many worn spots which read as white in the photograph; it was the dye which was the culprit. The pink fabric is in the best condition and was probably purchased for the quilt, since it is not pieced out the way the other colors are. The brown wool fabric was recycled from an earlier quilt or from clothing, for it has had more wear than the others. The olive green (used only in the outer border) and the black are both linen; both colors are pieced at least twice. The back is a loosely-woven wool, probably homespun.

$90.50. This was a large sum when measured against some of the other items.[1]

One wonders what one family was doing with that much material, living as they did in a tiny town on the frontier of Vermont. Nothing in the records indicates that he ran a store, though he could certainly have bought, sold and traded goods out of his home. A likelier explanation lies in the fact that, when they lived in Haverhill, John was a supplier of goods to the Continental Army. While he might have supplied almost anything, cloth for uniforms seems a good guess. If the end of the Revolution caught him with a large supply of material, it might have taken him a long time to sell off his inventory. Surely 243 yards of material is too much for household purposes; it is enough for a score of quilts.

Also listed in the inventory were two "bed quilts," one valued at $2.50 and another at $1.00. The will left his wife provided for; she received their house and some surrounding land for use during her natural life. She also received an annuity of 10 bushels of wheat and 20 bushels of Indian corn, as well as the use of one cow. On her death in 1818 at the age of 82, Catherine left no will; everything she had was deemed to be the property of her son Moody, with whom she lived out her life.

Abby Maria Hemenway, the great nineteenth-century collector and publisher of facts and odd information about Vermont, said, "Mrs. Catherine Sophia Rich was remarkable for industry, economy and liberality, as well as an accumulating faculty that filled her house with an abundance from which she dispensed with bountiful hand to those in need, none such going empty-handed from her door."[2]

1. Records of Essex County Probate Court, Guildhall, Vt.
2. Abby Maria Hemenway, *The Vermont Historical Gazetteer*, I (Burlington, Vt.: Miss A. M. Hemenway, 1868), p. 1031.

"Quilt as you go," "lap quilting" and "apartment quilting" describe the modern method of making a quilt in sections, without a frame. Abigail Seeger, in the 1860's, carried the method one step further: each block of her Rose of Sharon *is completely finished, bound edge and all, twenty-five miniature quilts (plus fill-in triangles) whipstitched together into a lovely traditional quilt.*

Abigail H. Stickney was born in Weybridge, Vermont in 1794. She married William Eldridge of nearby New Haven in 1812 and bore him five children. William died in 1835 and Abigail remained a widow until the last day of December 1849, when she married widower Gideon Seeger, Jr., of nearby Addison. The Stickneys, Eldridges and Seegers all settled in their respective towns well before 1800, creating farms in the fertile Lake Champlain valley.

Abigail's great-granddaughter remembers that her mother kept the Rose of Sharon *folded away in a dresser drawer, taking it out to display on the guest bed only when she entertained The Treasure Seekers, a missionary group of the First Baptist Church, or The Outlook Club, a local women's group.*

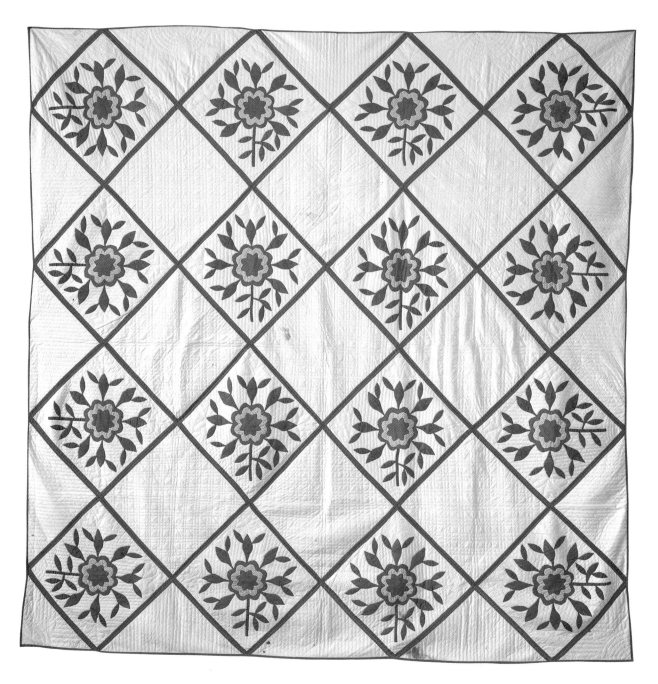

Rose of Sharon, *by Abigail Stickney Eldridge Seegar, Addison, c. 1850–1870, 96 x 100 inches, appliquéd cottons. Private collection, Vermont. #1013.*

Here was a woman with a different idea: one imagines her asking herself what the quilt would look like with a second color in the background blocks. It was a novel, and very successful, approach to a type of quilt which was almost always done on a white background. Besides being rather daring, Catharine Bolster was obviously possessed of a keen sense of color and design, a true artist in fabric. The signature block contains the place she lived (Barre, Vermont), the year she made it (1863) and her name; it also contains an uncommon bit of information, her date of birth (November 28, 1806).

While the addition of a vine, leaf and bud border to a pieced quilt is not particularly rare, the fact that it is appliquéd over those tan border triangles sets this quilt apart. The twelve muslin blocks are quilting samplers, each a different design.

Like others of our quiltmakers, Catharine married twice. She was not quite 21 when she married the first time, and was a widow of 42 when she wed her second husband.

Peony, by Catharine Graves Brockway Bolster, Barre, 1863, 100 x 80 inches, pieced and appliquéd cottons.
Private collection, Vermont. #1623.

RALLY 'ROUND THE FLAG, boys" comes from a northern song of the Civil War. American women on both sides of the Mason-Dixon Line also rallied 'round by doing their utmost for their respective war efforts. Apart from the necessity of running the farm, home and even business while the men were gone, women bore the brunt of relief work. The work of the United States Sanitary Commission, a private organization devoted to relief efforts on behalf of soldiers, is well documented. In the course of its life, upwards of seven thousand local women's groups aided its cause. Since bedding was one of the chief concerns in the hospitals, thousands of women contributed quilts to the cause. One twentieth-century researcher estimated that as many as a quarter of a million quilts and comforters were given by northern women alone.[15]

Laid end to end, those quilts would have stretched over 330 miles—from Philadelphia to Raleigh—something in excess of 40,000 bolts of fabric. One's mind struggles to take in the enormity of it—the co-ordination, the hours of labor, the sheer quantity of fabric. Mothers and grandmothers, sisters, cousins, aunts and sweethearts by the thousands were united in this labor of love and concern. Never before in wartime had quilts been so important, nor would they be in the future.

Many of the quilts contributed by women from the contending sides were made for that purpose, but others surely were family pieces, treasured by their owners. One imagines some tearful partings of owners from their quilts. Of course, the war did not consume all of the quilts produced north and south; if anything, the need for home consumption would have been greater than ever, because of the demand by the two armies for wool and cotton for uniforms and blankets. The scarcity of printed cottons for quilts led to more home spinning and weaving than in several decades.

Like other northerners, Vermonters were divided on the questions of abolitionism before the Civil War and Black

rights after it. They did, however, have very deep feelings about personal freedoms and individual liberty. Most Vermonters hoped war could be avoided; but, when it came, they were ready to do their part. For two decades prior to the war, Vermonters raised their voices in protest against slavery. The legislature sent dozens of petitions to Congress demanding the abolition of slavery and rejecting the admission of new slave states. Legislators instructed the state's Members of Congress to work for repeal of the Fugitive Slave Act and threatened with censure any who did not.[16]

Vermont took an anti-slavery stance early in its history. Its 1777 constitution outlawed slavery, the first in North America to do so. In the same year, a group of Vermont militia captured a British officer and his two slaves; after debating what to do, they voted to free the woman, Dinah Mattis, and her daughter. Their captain, Ebenezer Allen, wrote on the certificate, "I, being conscientious that it is not Right in the Sight of God to keep Slaves, I therefore, obtaining leave of the detachment under my command, I give her and her child their freedom."[17] Here was a spontaneous dem-

Courtesy of The Northfield Historical Society.

✳

In the late afternoon of a fine summer's day in 1898, Homer Howe (foreground) and a friend lead the cows home beside the Center Park in Northfield. Even families which were not farm dwellers, such as the Howes, frequently kept one or two cows for their own use. In an age before America became diet-conscious, Jersey cows like this pair were valued for the high butterfat content of their milk. Now most Vermont dairy cows are Holsteins, which produce far higher quantities of milk than the Jerseys, but with a much lower butterfat content.

onstration of the love of liberty so characteristic of Vermonters.

Sixty years later, a New York slave owner sued in Vermont courts to recover an escaped slave being har-bored there. Judge Theophilus Harrington denied the request, as there was no proof of ownership; he would accept nothing less, he said, than "a bill of sale from the Almighty."[18]

In 1856, in the midst of the turmoil and bloodshed in Kansas over whether that territory would be admitted as a free or a slave state, a group of Vermonters who went west to bolster the Free State forces were attacked by pro-slavery forces. Their homes were burned and many of their possessions were lost. When news reached Vermont, the legislature voted to send $20,000 (a very large sum in those days) to Kansas for the relief of the former Vermonters. The money was received—and returned with thanks and a note, that while the Free Staters appreciated the thought, they could get along without help, and would prefer to.[19] The folks at home would have said it was characteristic for Vermonters to be so self-reliant.

President Lincoln's call for troops found Vermont ready to help. One week after Lincoln's telegram arrived, the legislature met in special session; the next day, it voted $500,000 for war expenses, with another half-million on call. Compared with previous state spending, the sum was enormous: in 1860, the total of all state, county and town taxes raised in Vermont was $900,000. It also marked the first time that the state borrowed for its expenditures, a big step in a state accustomed to buying only what it had cash in hand to pay for. Before war's end, two more million dollars followed the first; it took until 1879 to pay off the war debt.[20]

Vermont's 240 towns and cities each did its part to help. Over $5,000,000 was raised by the people themselves, who voted in their town or city meetings to tax themselves to support the war. Banks, businesses and wealthy citizens gave hundreds of thousands more, and even Vermont-born residents of other states sent contributions back to the Green Mountains.[21]

Vermont woolen mills, using fleeces from those famous Merinos, churned out material for uniforms for the state's first regiments. A group of 200 Burlington women adopted a resolution which stated, "We further resolve that we will consider *All* our time and *All* our energies sacred to this object." On May 25, 1861, 25 days after Lincoln's call for troops, the First Regiment of Vermont Volunteers left Rutland, bound for Fortress Monroe, Virginia. Most of these men were members of existing militia companies and so had some training; the vast majority of those who came after them were raw recruits. On their departure, each man of the First bore in his cap a sprig of evergreen, a symbol by which their ancestors, the Green Mountain Boys, had distinguished themselves. This became the trademark of Vermont troops throughout the war.[22]

From a population of 315,000, Vermont sent 34,328 men to the war, most of them as volunteers. (By contrast, fewer than half that number served in

▷ *This quilt is said to have been made from Mary Eastman Tillotson's wedding dress. If so, she was a fortunate bride to have been wed in a fine roller-plated glazed chintz, probably of English manufacture. The chintz reminds us that, even as late as the middle of the nineteenth century, Americans were still dependent to a large extent upon the factories of England and France for the finer grades of cloth (made, as likely as not, from American cotton).*

While this might strike a modern viewer as a dark garment for a wedding gown, it is important to remember that, after the wedding was over, the dress was expected to lead a long life. From the condition of the quilt, it is evident that if Mary Tillotson did wear the dress after the wedding, she was very careful. Putting worn-out garments into quilts is a tradition of long-standing, but to find one like this, of such fine — and probably expensive — fabric, is rather rare in Vermont. If its maker couldn't bear the thought of wearing out such a lovely piece of cloth, Vermont frugality wouldn't allow her just to leave it in storage. A quilt provided the logical way to use the material before it was worn and washed to tatters. The resulting quilt was surely kept for best, reserved for such occasions of state as a visit from the minister or the sewing group or the better-off relatives from down country.

The fabric itself presents us with another question. None of the four strips is over 24 inches wide, making it narrower by several inches that the fabric generally available at the time of the wedding (about 1840). One wonders if the fabric wasn't purchased a decade or two earlier and then never used.

The Tillotsons themselves are the subject of an interesting story. In their 96th year (1905), Mary and Jonathan won a prize offered by the Boston Post for the oldest married couple in New England. Their prize was a pair of armchairs, which Mary lived to enjoy another six years. At her death in October 1911, she was 102 years old.

World War I.[23]) Wounds or disease claimed 5,237 lives,[24] but the total would have been much higher had it not been for an innovation devised by Vermonters at home. Alarmed by the number of deaths of wounded soldiers, people at home found a new method of caring for the men. Starting in 1862, the state sent agents to the front to select those strong enough to be sent home for care in Vermont hospitals. This procedure was so successful — 75% of the men brought home eventually went back to the front lines — that it was later adopted by other states.[25]

The war lay heavily on the minds of the women at home, and they revealed their concern in the quilts they kept. Patriotic motifs were popular during the period, as were memorial quilts to the men who went to war. Two of the quilts presented here bear dates from the middle year of the Civil War, 1863, but only one makes any reference to the great conflict.

Jane A. Stickle's quilt (page 60) is a poignant reminder of the anguish of those left at home. Its inscription leaves no doubt as to what was on her

mind: "In War Time 1863 / Pieces 5,602 / Jane A. Stickle." The quilt is breathtaking in its complexity. Many of its 225 square and triangular blocks are original designs, each requiring its own pattern and template, each requiring patient calculations to get the mathematics right. The small size of the blocks and pieces also seems to have been a deliberate attempt to occupy time. This quilt obviously took her a lifetime to make, compressed into the four war years; it is worth a lifetime of tears.

Catharine Bolster, on the other hand, maker of the *Peony* quilt (page 35), gave no evidence in her work of concern for the war. The inscription reads, "Barre Vt. 1863 / Catharine Bolster / born Nov. 28th 1806." She may have made one or two or more of those 250,000 Sanitation Commission quilts, or perhaps she volunteered some of her time each week to work at the army hospital in Montpelier, just seven miles from her Barre home. The Bolster quilt tells us that even in the midst of national passion and drama, life went on at home.

Whole Cloth, by Mary Eastman Tillotson, Orange, c. 1840–1850, 91½ x 95 inches, pieced cottons.
Collection of The Vermont Historical Society. #110.

FROM THE COMPROMISE OF 1850, the last best effort of Henry Clay and Daniel Webster to preserve the union, to the Spanish-American War in 1898, America raced through the second half of the nineteenth century determined to do something good, to get somewhere fast, to become a nation to be noticed and reckoned with.

From the harbingers of war in the 1850's, the Kansas-Nebraska Act, the Dred Scott Decision and John Brown's Raid, north and south marched steadily, perhaps unstoppably, toward civil strife. Some on both sides welcomed it, but most Americans dreaded the prospect. When war did come, neither side was prepared; each expected something of short duration. None but a Cassandra would have predicted the long, bloody devastation which followed.

At war's end, both sides were physically, emotionally and financially exhausted. The political divisions, exacerbated in part by the decade of reconstruction in the south, probably never healed completely. In one small respect, the south could be said to have triumphed in the end for, starting in the 1920's, many northern firms, especially textile companies, were lured south by promises of cheap labor. The migration affected Vermont, too, where labor costs had been the lowest in New England.[26]

Westward expansion, which never stopped entirely during the Civil War, continued at a greater pace than ever, aided by completion of the first transcontinental railroad in 1869. More of the plains states and the west were opened to settlement as other rail lines were completed. One of these was the Northern Pacific, built by Vermonter Frederick Billings, for whom the Montana city is named. He was one of the thousands of Vermonters lured to California by the gold rush, but he made his first fortune as San Francisco's first lawyer.[27] Mechanical improvements and inventions of every sort helped American farmers become the most productive in the world. Immigrants from around the world poured into the vast land by the millions, though

many got no farther west than the western edge of cities on the eastern seaboard.

America at the Centennial of 1876 was full of itself, brash, boasting, proud. Proud of its growing importance in world affairs and certain of even greater successes, the nation wanted to meet the world as an equal. Americans rode to the tops of taller and taller buildings made possible by the elevators invented by Vermont native Elisha Otis. Their tastes and opinions began to be molded by advertising agencies, the first of which was started in Boston in 1865 by Vermonter George Presbury Rowell, who later moved his agency to New York City. Thousands of American parlors sported reed organs built in Brattleboro, Vermont, by Jacob Estey. Listeners around the world thrilled—or cringed—to the sounds of the steam calliope invented by Vermont native Joshua Stoddard.

From the 1880's and well into the next century, small-town life across America and in Vermont was enlivened by traveling actors, lecturers and singers. Even the tiniest hamlet could, if it had a hall, expect to receive visits from these performers. Lectures on the horrors of Andersonville Prison, declamations from Shakespeare, trained animal acts and mixtures of popular and classical music all came to the state. This much the railroads did, at least, to broaden the horizons of nineteenth-century Americans.

American industry, American agriculture, American science pointed the way to a better world.

There were numerous scandals; the Grant administration was an embarrassment to many, but Americans then were perhaps more inured to graft and corruption by public figures. Mark Twain characterized it as an age which was gilded, not gold. As big business grew bigger, some of it grew more greedy, and an era commenced in which some corporations exercised more power than state governments. One of those was the oil industry, begun in 1850 when Vermonter Edwin Drake drilled America's first oil well in Pennsylvania.

Though there was greater abundance in the land, in some respects the lives of ordinary citizens in 1900 were not much improved over those of 1850. Hard times and financial panics in 1853, 1873 and 1893 ravaged a good share of the population, especially small businesses and farmers. Many of these people had good reason to wonder whether the new century would be kinder to them than the old.

Vermonters, too, might have asked themselves that question. After the growth of the state from 154,000 in 1800 to 314,000 in 1850, population increases virtually stopped; in the next fifty years, Vermont added just 28,500 people.[28] Out-migration continued to be a concern. In 1902, *The Vermonter* magazine estimated that 169,000 people born in Vermont then

Whig Rose, *unknown maker, Dorset, c. 1850–1870, 76 x 78 inches, pieced and appliquéd cottons.*
Collection of Hugh and Mary Kent Onion. #2679.

lived outside the state, compared with 248,000 natives still left among the Green Mountains.[29] People at home took this very much to heart: "[Long] did the hill farmers mourn the departing young in heart who were not satisfied to harvest rocks."[30]

No doubt about it, Vermont *is* a rocky place, and hard to plow. When the best farm land was used up, when sheep no longer produced fleeces of gold, when commodity prices were low, the sons and daughters of Vermont farms left those farms for other opportunities. Not all left the state, of course; some became town or city dwellers, taking up town or city occupations. For those left on the home places, dairy cows succeeded sheep as the producers of whatever money there was to be made on the farm. At first it was butter and cheese, but what saved such farms as were left was the ever-expanding eastern seaboard, with its demand for milk. Vermont milk went by train to Boston and New York in ever-increasing quantities, and today these places remain the principal market for Vermont dairy farmers.

As the great social upheavals of the first half of the century reached their conclusion with the Civil War, society, religion and politics began to retrench in Vermont. Whereas the state was known before the Civil War as a radical place, in the hundred years afterward it developed a well-deserved reputation for conservatism.

The Republican ascendancy in Vermont was assured because of its image as the party which put down the "War of the Rebellion" (as it was still called here as late as 1902). Its power was unbroken for over a hundred years (save for the freak Congressional election of 1958 which sent a liberal Democrat to the U.S. House). Its leaders were businessmen, just as the national leaders were and, though big business in Vermont was tiny by comparison, they were businessmen nonetheless.

Mrs. Alfred Joseph Fletcher of Lyndonville scatters feed for her chickens in the farm yard. Farm wives often maintained flocks of laying hens, obtaining some cash income by selling eggs.

From Vermont Album — A Collection of Early Vermont Photographs, *ed. Ralph Nading Hill, Copyright ©1974 by The Stephen Greene Press. Used by permission. (Negative number AQZ 4.)*

I T IS SOMETIMES DIFFICULT TO tell whether the Vermonters who left or the Vermonters who stayed were the more fervent in their praise of the state. Stephen A. Douglas, a native of Brandon, got himself into hot water back home by asserting that Vermont was a fine place to be from, provided you left at an early age and never returned. (The remark may account in part for the shellacking he took in his home state in the 1860 presidential election.)

For many who left, Vermont exerted a powerful tug on the emotions. Across the United States and even abroad, these émigrés organized "Vermont Societies" and "Sons (or Daughters) of Vermont." Their meetings were occasions for toasting the state of their birth and recounting fond memories of their growing-up days. In later years, many returned for visits; they found Old Home Day celebrations organized by Vermonters eager to cash in on the phenomenon.[31] Hardship and deprivation were forgotten in a golden glow of nostalgia, to be replaced by bowdlerized memories of harmony with nature and near-perfect Yankee upbringings.

Not every Vermonter who went away promoted education, temperance or religion, or died loved—or at least respected—by all. Some emigrants were notorious rather than famous.

Horace Austin Warner Tabor went west with a long-suffering wife and small child, failing first at homesteading in Kansas before moving to Colorado to join in the Pike's Peak gold rush. By luck rather than by labor, he ended up owner or part owner in several rich mines and became known as Silver Dollar Tabor. He was mayor of Leadville, drank and gambled to excess, built opera houses in Denver and Leadville, "and always passed out money lavishly to moochers of every degree." He served as Colorado's Lieutenant Governor and used part of his fortune to persuade the state legislature to elect him to the United States Senate to fill the thirty days remaining in an unexpired term. Along the way he divorced his hard-working first wife

and married a beautiful divorcée known as Baby Doe. He ended his life as Denver's postmaster, stone broke. Author Stewart Holbrook calls him Colorado's favorite legend, but says primly that the ex-Vermonter "accomplished little or nothing of lasting influence."[32]

Another legendary figure was the Brattleboro-born financier and meddler-in-railroads, Jim Fisk, who began his career as a peddler of tinware in northern New England. Success carried him to New York City, where he launched himself into finance on a grander scale, in a field where the potential profits far exceeded those available to a tin peddler. In 1869, Fisk and Jay Gould nearly succeeded in an attempt to corner the gold market. Their failure helped blacken the reputation of officials of the Grant administration. He was also mixed up in attempts to water the stock of New York's Erie Railroad. Such escapades put him very much in the public eye and made him a target for attacks by newspaper editors and cartoonists. Even in an era of unrestrained capitalism, Fisk was excessive, his chicanery remarkable for its breadth and depth.[33]

One of the state's most notorious exports was Sile (born Silas) Doty. He claimed to have burgled more houses, escaped from more jails and stolen more property than any other person in his time (1800-1876). While the boast might have been true, one writer said of him that he "was an artist at crime but not too successful a practitioner of it." On his death, the newspaper in Angola, Indiana (scene of many of his escapades), splashed the following headline across its front page: "THE LAST OF SILAS DOTY!— Death of a Wonderful Man—What an Eventful Life!"[34] No one ever said a Vermonter lacked ingenuity.

For some Vermonters, leaving the state was never an option to be considered. For reasons they themselves might have been unable to understand, much less explain, they stayed, rooted to the soil by a feeling of belonging, by a sense of being someone unique, of being a Vermonter. Today there are still people who farm the land cleared by their ancestors five, six and even

seven generations ago, and who stand for continuity in the face of change. Two of these families are the Ballards of Georgia and the Palmers of Waitsfield.

In the spring of 1788, Joseph Ballard purchased 100 acres of land in Georgia, Vermont, from Ira Allen's Onion River Land Company. Two hundred years later, the sixth generation of Ballards continue to farm the land, which now numbers 610 acres. About 1835, high prices for the wool they raised enabled a descendant to graft an imposing brick house onto the modest frame structure which had stood for many years. There it was that one of the Ballard women made the *LeMoyne Star* with diagonal stripes quilt (page 19).

A quarter-century after the Ballards settled in Georgia, Erastus Allen left Massachusetts for Waitsfield. There, on the spine of the Green Mountains, in what is now a ski resort town, he cleared land and about 1812 built the house in which his descendants still live. Several times since Erastus Allen died the farm passed to the eldest daughter, a tradition the present owners hope to continue. Then as now, farming was an occupation which made few people rich; often both men and women had to find other ways to supplement farm earnings. Jennie Barnard Palmer, Erastus Allen's granddaughter, maker of the *Nine Patch* variation quilt (page 45), made straw hats at home. Her earnings went toward installing pipes for running water in her home; the Palmer farm was one of the first in town to have this late-nineteenth-century luxury.

Vermonters who remained on the farms or in the villages carried on as best they could. The sheep which brought such prosperity also caused damage; widespread over-grazing led to loss of groundcover and extensive soil erosion. Photos from the 1840's through the 1880's show hillsides denuded of trees, and fields where rocks show through like skeletons. Some towns shriveled up; abandoned farmhouses and barns fell in upon themselves, much crop and pasture land was reclaimed by brush, and the sheep-fed prosperity of the first half of the nineteenth century faded into memory.

Lura Clapp Allen was born in Grand Isle, Vermont, in the spring of 1791, just as Vermont was relinquishing its status as an independent republic to become the fourteenth state. In 1812, she was married to Joel Allen, nephew of Grand Isle's first settler. Joel was a self-educated and highly respected member of the community, a natural leader. When the British invaded nearby Plattsburg, New York, in 1814, Joel gathered together seventeen of his neighbors. They rowed across Lake Champlain, fought with distinction and rowed back. Lura, in later years, often told the story of hearing the great cannons as she was milking the cows, hoping that her young husband was all right.*

Lura was sixty years old when she made her Sunburst quilt. Her quilt is obviously the work of a talented and experienced needlewoman, with many small pieces carefully fitted together. The quilting is close and very fine, twelve to fourteen stitches in each inch. Lura was justifiably proud of her quilt, and stitched her initials and the date, to mark it as her own.

The Sunburst now belongs to another Lura, great-great-granddaughter of the maker.

*Allen Stratton, History of the Town of North Hero, Vermont, (Burlington, Vt.: George Little Press, 1976), pp. 182–183. This story is also in the files of Lucy L. Allen Wells, as reported to the Quiltsearch Committee in a letter of October 23, 1989.

Sunburst, by Lura Clapp Allen, North Hero, 1851, 82 x 85 inches, pieced cottons.
Collection of Lura Allen Carr. #1242.

Maple sugar — you couldn't just go to the store and buy that staple of Vermont cooking if you lived in Illinois. And you were sure to be homesick for it; that little bit of hard brown sugar had a distinctive flavor that brought back clear memories of late nights spent "sugaring off" when a perfect spring day made the sap run in gallons. What would you do? Why, send for some, of course.

Fred and Jennie Palmer were not among the young families who moved west. They stayed right on the family farm in Waitsfield, Vermont, a farm Jennie inherited from her mother. And, as part of their busy farm life, they produced and sold maple sugar.

Sometime in 1880, someone decided that it would be fun to collect the signatures of all those maple-sugar customers, now spread from Waitsfield and Moretown and Fayston to upstate New York and further west to Silver Lake, Minnesota, and Middle Creek, Illinois, and other small towns in the midwest. Small slips of fabric went out with the orders that year, and with the fabric went instructions to sign it, to write down the new home town and to return it to Jennie, because she was going to make a quilt.

Many of those customers did as Jennie asked — some, like members of the Comer family in Cosmos, Minnesota, added the date (December 23, 1880) and others added ages as well (Peter Drew, Waitsfield, 83 years old). Jennie did make a quilt, a simple but pleasing pattern, with plain quilting, nothing fancy. After all, it was the names that were important. And today Jennie's quilt is on the same farm, where the sixth and seventh generations of the family still live, continuing the traditions of their ancestors.

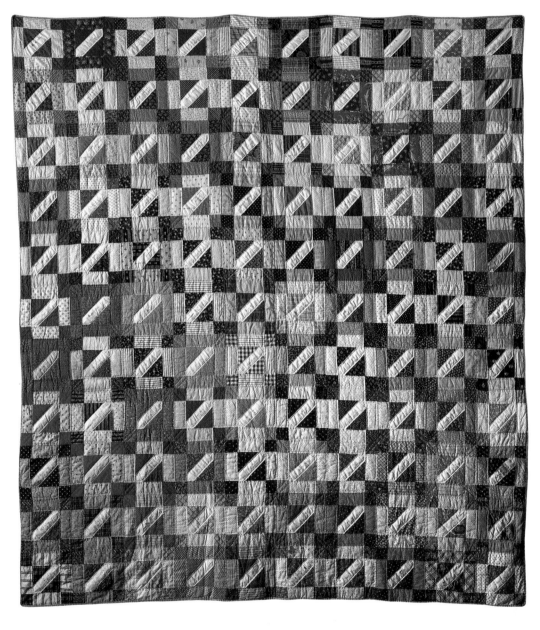

Nine Patch *variation, by Jennie Barnard Palmer, Waitsfield, c. 1880–1885, 83 x 92 inches, pieced cottons.*
Collection of Fred and Josette Messer. #2098.

Abandonment of some of the hill farms led to consolidation of many of the remaining ones and, though the number of farms declined, their overall acreage increased. The people who stayed were not without resources or resourcefulness; Vermonters are, after all, an inventive lot, and it took a lot of inventiveness to tease a living from the rocky soil. Salvation for many came with a change from sheep to dairy cattle. Cattle were by no means new to Vermont; they were present in large numbers for decades prior to the Civil War, but these were largely beef animals raised for shipment out of state. Some farmers diversified, adding other kinds of livestock, such as horses, oxen, chickens or pigs; for many, maple syrup was an important cash crop. Others set up small shops at home for manufacturing or repairs, or even for small-scale retail sales. For most Vermont farmers after the Civil War, though, the dairy cow was the ticket to survival.

As the demand grew for milk and butter along the populous eastern seaboard, Vermont farmers produced and shipped more and more; the state became as famous for its dairy products in the late 1800's as it had been for its sheep fifty years earlier. Herds grew while the human population stayed the same or declined; by the 1920's, Vermont was the only state in the country to have more cows than people, an oft-quoted and much-laughed-about situation which continued until 1963.[35]

As Vermont approaches the twenty-first century, there are fewer dairy farms each year. In 1945, Vermonters operated 26,490 farms; by 1980, the number had plummeted to 3,209, and it continues to drop.[36] It is not so much the fact that farming is hard seven-days-a-week work, but the spiraling costs which discourage many sons and daughters. The costs of machinery, feed and taxes combine to push many farms over that thin line between black and red ink.

That Vermonters continue to operate ancestral farms is a tribute to those virtues of patience, persistence and hard work. It is also something which is harder to quantify, that feeling of being a breed apart and of a sense of place which comes from having so many generations of ancestors who lived here. It is partly this feeling which held, and continues to hold, many young Vermonters when their friends and relatives left the state for the promised lands outside its borders. It is this feeling which persuades many people that Vermont is, indeed, a particularly special place in which to live.

From Vermont Album – A Collection of Early Vermont Photographs, *ed. Ralph Nading Hill, Copyright ©1974 by The Stephen Greene Press. Used by permission.*

Jennie Barnard Palmer, maker of the album quilt on page 45, was one of many Vermont women who wove straw hats to add to the family income. Contractors furnished prepared palm leaves to their weavers and returned later to collect the completed hats. It was no small business, either. One southern Vermont entrepreneur worked with two hundred weavers who supplied him with twenty thousand hats each year. This photograph (negative number ATX 622), taken in Windham County between 1890 and 1910, shows part of that harvest of hats.

J AMES WILSON OF BRADFORD, Vermont, a farmer by trade, embodied three of Vermont's cardinal virtues—inventiveness, hard work and persistence (and, of course, the ability to make money, though this was usually called "thrift"). In 1796 he saw at Dartmouth College two globes, a sight which fascinated and even obsessed him.

Deciding to replicate them, he first turned on a home lathe the necessary wooden spheres, but bumped up against a lack of some of the specialized knowledge also required. By turns he sold some of his livestock to buy a set of the *Encyclopedia Britannica* (for $130, a very large sum in those days), walked to New Haven, Connecticut (by way of Boston and Newburyport, Massachusetts) to learn copper engraving, and finally trekked to Charlestown, Massachusetts, to be tutored by a famous geographer.

At the end of fourteen years of toil, he sold a pair of his globes for $50. (Yankee that he was, he also manufactured their wooden bases, brass quadrants and shipping boxes.) His work was praised and sought after and, because business was so good, he moved, to Albany, New York. Wilson continued to tinker and invent and perfect things until well after his eightieth birthday, as his globes continued to sell and to bring praise for their inventor.[37]

Geography also interested Emma Marcy Worden, who was not quite twenty-four when she completed her map of Windham County, Vermont (page 89). It records in meticulous detail the shape of each town and its settlements, as accurate a record as any map on paper. Perhaps Mrs. Worden used that standard reference of Vermont counties, *Beer's Atlas*, whose various volumes were published during the 1870's. There she would have found just the information she needed.

To be a farm family in Vermont in the 1890's did not mean one was cut off from the world nor ignorant of its events. There was always an almanac available for forecasts about the weather, for advice on household matters, for guesstimates about the best

Crazy quilt, by Cecile Sullens Depoutee, Middlebury, c. 1889–1891, 88 x 76 inches, pieced and appliquéd silks, satins, failles and velvets. Collection of Judy C. Young. #2448.

times for fishing. There would surely have been a Bible, maybe a few volumes of nineteenth-century favorites such as Stevenson, Cooper and Irving, and maybe some Twain. Nearby Brattleboro's daily paper reached into Guilford, carrying news of the small town's doings, its births, deaths, marriages, as well as of the great outside world. Emma Marcy's schooling might have been rudimentary, but she would have been able to read, write and do sums—and possibly much more. Lack of extensive formal training did not by any means condemn the Vermonter to a life of ignorance; the interested and persistent person could keep on learning all of his or her life.

But why, one asks, make a map of one county? Why not the whole state of Vermont? Why not all of New England? It might simply have been that Windham County was what Emma Worden knew best, and so she decided to stick with what she knew. Whatever her motivation, it is plain from her quilt that for her geography, like charity, began at home.

Cecile Sullens Depoutee, on the other hand, took a broader, albeit different, view of matters. This British-born resident of Middlebury might have felt she needed a little tutoring about the United States (or that her children or grandchildren did). What better or more effective way to learn the states than to make a quilt about them? Mrs. Depoutee's quilt (opposite) is a catalogue of the states rather than a map.

Fortunately for Mrs. Depoutee, the number of states corresponded nicely with a round number for blocks—seven down, six across. There was nothing untidy about the number of states, no odd number which would have meant some furious figuring to get it to come out right. The blocks themselves are delicate pieces of work, many with flowers and other embellishments. There doesn't appear to have been any attempt to put in state flowers, a kind of quilt which became popular some years later. Neither are the states listed in any particular order.

Cecile Depoutee's Middlebury was a thriving town, the commercial center for much of a county rich in farmland and small industry and home to the

◁ Cecile Sullens Depoutee used most of the techniques and materials known to quiltmakers when she created this wonderful crazy quilt a century ago. Like other women of the period who wielded needles, she cross-stitched, embroidered, pieced and appliquéd the surface of this quilt. She also twisted narrow grosgrain ribbon and used paints to achieve the desired effect. The beauty and complexity of the work suggest that its maker had considerable practice before she began this quilt.

From the middle 1870's through the half-century which followed, American women made hundreds of thousands of crazy quilts. The typical example was a riot of fabrics and sewing techniques, an opportunity for a quiltmaker—or a person who did not ordinarily make quilts—to show off her best work and fanciest stitches. While this quilt contains most of the standard features of its species, it differs in two respects—its large size (big enough to cover a bed), and the fact that each of the 42 ten-inch blocks is named for one of the United States.

Perhaps the quilt was a geography lesson for its maker, who was born in England about 1840, or for her children or grandchildren. It might also have been inspired by the admission to the union, in the period from 1888 to 1890, of several of the plains and western states. Some state names are painted, others are embroidered, some are cross-stitched and still others are rendered in twisted ribbon. Kansas shows up as a photograph of the state capitol on a satin ribbon.

Cecile Sullens Depoutee was an artist who worked in more than one medium; she painted on fabric, was a wood carver and created pictures and shadow boxes of floral arrangements from the hair of family members. There is little additional information about her; in the 1920's, her family fell victim to scarlet fever, and most of the paper records were burned to retard the spread of the disease. The maker herself lived less than a decade after completing her quilt; she died in 1899.

illustrious college. As a college town, it was—and still is—a hub of cultural and intellectual activity, the site of lectures and plays. Standing as it does halfway between the two principal cities of the state, astride the main north-south highway, it sees a good share of Vermont come and go, as well as many out-of-state visitors. One didn't have to exert oneself very much to find out what was going on in the world during these first two years of Benjamin Harrison's administration. (There was some local interest in that administration; after all, Vice President Levi P. Morton was a native of Shoreham, hardly a dozen miles down the road.) No, while Emma Worden might have had to work a little harder to bring the world to Guilford, all Cecile Depoutee had to do was wait and a good share of the world would pass by her door.

Interested in the world, Vermonters have always made much of education, talking about it a good deal (still a popular pastime), and even going so far as to enshrine it in the first Vermont constitution.

That radical document, which forbade slavery and allowed men to vote without the requirements for property prevalent in other states, also called for the establishment of schools from the primary level through a state-chartered university. American schools in this period were often crude affairs, sometimes holding sessions only at times when the children were not needed at home. Teachers were often ill-prepared, sometimes barely more than children themselves, and supplies were few and frequently shoddy. Even New England, which was generally ahead of the rest of the country in education, had a long way to go.

It took some time for the state to make its 1777 vision a reality, but Vermonters, sharing the New England tradition of literacy and respect for education, carried this legacy with them as they moved across the continent. A good many of them ended up in education, sometimes by intent and sometimes by accident.

Local records across the nation are filled with the names of Vermonters who either started the first school or

In September, 1910, teacher Inez Woodbury and her first-grade class pose for a photograph in the Northfield Graded School. Built in 1876, the structure served for a time as the town's high school and continues in use to the present day, looking very much as it did eighty years ago.

were the first teachers in it. In Akron, Ohio, it was the Reverend Isaac Jennings, whose system was later adopted across most of Ohio. In 1847 the first school in St. Paul, Minnesota, was started by Miss Harriet Bishop, who also made a name for herself later as a temperance agitator. When emigrants from the Green Mountains planted a whole new colony, as they did at Vermontville, Michigan, in the 1830's, they meticulously organized the schools from bottom to top.[38]

The Vermonters did not limit their efforts to elementary and secondary schools; many colleges were founded by the peripatetic émigrés. One of the earliest, and certainly the most influ-

ential in much of the midwest and west, was Ohio's Oberlin College. It was founded in 1833 by two graduates of Vermont's Pawlet Academy, Philo Penfield Stewart and John Jay Shipherd, both Congregational preachers. Oberlin was the first American college to admit women and Blacks. Many of its graduates went on to become missionaries or educators (often both) in other parts of the country, scattering

schools and colleges in their wake. (Founder Stewart was nothing if not versatile; his improved cooking stove sold by the thousands in the old Northwest Territory and made a good deal of money for the college.[39]) Other colleges founded by Vermonters were Grinnell in Iowa (Josiah Bushnell Grinnell, to whom Horace Greeley — once an apprentice in a Vermont printshop — addressed his famous remark

At first glance, one might consign this graceful tulip to the 1920's or 1930's, since it so resembles one of the kit quilts of that period. The quilt was actually made prior to the 1865 wedding of Martha Jane Hulett. Its subdued colors were once the brilliant red and green combination popular from the 1850's to the 1870's, with a touch of orange thrown in. Unstable dyes faded the red petals to tan. Unlike many floral patterns, these tulips are very lifelike (contrast this quilt with the one on page 65 for an entirely different look in tulips).

Martha Jane Hulett Culver's quiltmaking career spanned more than fifty years, from this quilt (and earlier, one suspects, judging from the quality of the work) to 1910, when her eyesight finally failed her. The quilt remains in the hands of her granddaughter, who lives in the farmhouse where the quilt was made.

Tulip, by Martha Jane Hulett Culver, Pawlet, c. 1860–1865, 80 x 80 inches, pieced and appliquéd cottons.
Collection of Mildred E. O'Neal. #215.

about going west), Mills in California (by Susan Lincoln Tolman Mills) and Kalamazoo in Michigan (by Nathaniel Balch).[40]

The state sent forth many sons and daughters to head up already established colleges: among these were Milo Jewett, first president of Vassar; Webster Merrifield, University of South Dakota; Charles Kendall Adams, Cornell and the University of Wisconsin; Lucien Berry at DePauw; and George A. Gates, president in turn of Iowa College, Pomona College and Fiske College for Negroes.[41]

Two Vermonters who profoundly influenced education in this country were Justin Smith Morrill and John Dewey. As a congressman from Vermont, Morrill introduced the Land Grant Colleges Act in 1862, opening the way to the establishment of many of America's state universities and giving to untold numbers of Americans a chance for higher education. Dewey was graduated from the University of Vermont, and at twenty-three left the state. As a writer and theorist on educational matters in the early twentieth century, Dewey was without peer,

though certainly not without critics.

Stewart Holbrook, chronicler of the migration of New Englanders to the rest of the nation, says of the educators, "Here was New England's great and incomparable export." There was hardly a locality in the United States unacquainted with, or unaffected by, the Yankee schoolteacher. "From the metropolis of New York to the far reaches of Montana and Texas, to the back counties of Arkansas and Georgia, to say nothing of Alaska and Hawaii, or even of Asia and Africa, the figure of the Yankee schoolteacher has found his or her way, and left an impression, no matter how small or confined."[42]

Vermonter Samuel Read Hall, a resident of Concord, established the modern system of teacher training in 1823 when he founded a teachers' seminary in Concord. His Columbian School was the first of its kind in America, and its curriculum, along with the principles laid down by Hall in his book *Lectures on School Keeping*, helped shape education for generations. Hall was also a pioneer in the use of the blackboard.[43]

One of the products of Hall's efforts might very well have been the woman we know only as Lizzie, a teacher in Randolph, Vermont, in the middle 1850's. It was for her that the friendship quilt top (page 55) was made. Four of the signers identified themselves as pupils; one called herself "Your little scholar." Ten blocks contain sayings or short poems, some of which allude to partings, so one suspects that Lizzie was leaving the school, if not the state. It seems likely that some of the students themselves moved away; four of the signatures carry New York place names, three from Massachusetts, and one even from Illinois. In some cases several people with the same surname signed, whole families of students and parents.

Whoever she was, wherever she went, Lizzie was held in obvious esteem and affection by the people who signed her quilt top. One inscription in particular sums it up—indeed, speaks to the subject of friendship quilts generally: Abby P. McIntire wrote, "Distance cannot separate hearts united by friendship." The anonymous Lizzie, forgotten but for her going-away present, stands for all those Vermonters, men and women, who went forth from the Green Mountains to preach the gospel of education. Jane W. McIntire could have had them in mind when she wrote, "To teach us to remember our days that we may apply our hearts unto wisdom."

Adelbert M. Corser, an amateur photographer who took many pictures of everyday life in his hometown of Putney, was the proprietor of the general store on the far right in this photograph taken around 1900. The village store in rural communities served as grocery, pharmacy, social center and, of course, source of fabric and notions for quiltmakers.

Lois A. Page Halbert was halfway through her life when she made this wonderful quilt. In its 42 blocks appear a whole Vermont summer garden, from violets to roses. Though its colors are now faded, what a bright and cheerful garden it must have been.

Each bouquet or wreath is meticulously crafted, sometimes from several layers of appliqué, and each block bears in ink the name of the flower or flowers. The vine-and-leaf border is a masterpiece of mathematics, awe-inspiring in its complexity and precision. Unfortunately, because most of the flowers have faded and the vine and leaves have not, the border now overpowers the rest. In spite of this present imbalance, Lois Halbert created a work of art.

Of the quiltmaker herself, little is known; she was born in Cambridge, Vermont, in 1825 and died in Essex, Vermont, in 1891, aged 66. The signature block (the wreath in the fourth row down) reads, "Lois A. Halbert Essex, Vt. Aged 33." The quilt passed to a cousin with whom she lived and worked during the summers and is now owned by a granddaughter of that cousin.

Floral appliqué sampler, by Lois A. Page Halbert, Essex, 1858, 86 x 86 inches, pieced and appliquéd cottons.
Collection of Mrs. John Scanlon. #702.

"If while on earth we have to part—
And move to far off distant lands,
If friendship has entwined the heart,
Distance can never break the bands."

So wrote William C. Richardson on his block for this album quilt, believed to have been made for a Randolph schoolteacher in 1856, perhaps on the occasion of her marriage. We know that her name was Elizabeth (two inscriptions mention "Dear Lizzie"), that she was a teacher (several signatures are prefaced by "your pupil"), and that she was leaving the area (numerous references to distance, partings and adieus).

But where did she go? Was she part of the great westward migration of Vermonters in the mid-nineteenth century? Or was she moving a shorter distance, to set up housekeeping as a newlywed near her husband's family? Was she sad to go, or did she relish the adventure? When she got there, was her new life all she had hoped for?

All we know is that Lizzie's quilt top, never quilted, appeared more than one hundred years later in an old barn in North Brookfield, Massachusetts. The barn belonged to sons of J. R. Southworth, one of the signers of Lizzie's top. How her quilt came to be there, and whatever happened to Lizzie, remain topics for speculation.

Friendship album quilt top, unknown maker, Randolph, c. 1856–1860, 58 x 66 inches, pieced cottons.
Collection of Randolph Historical Society, Inc. #2160.

ENTERPRISING WOMEN

IN AN AGE WHEN WOMEN WORK ON CONSTRUCTION SITES and men work as nurses, the thought of women running businesses hardly occasions a second thought — if it warrants even a first one. This represents a considerable and quite recent change in attitude in a country which bestowed on women the general right to vote only seventy years ago.

As women began to seek professions outside the home, there were some types of jobs deemed suitable, such as teaching or factory work. By 1846, over 1,200 young Vermont women were working in the textile mills in Lowell, Massachusetts, a pattern which continued for many years.[1] For a woman to start a business, or even to take over one already running, was not particularly common, especially in the nineteenth century.

Still, there were exceptions to every rule. One of the most famous business women of the last century was Lydia Estes Pinkham, born in Lynn, Massachusetts, in 1819. She was the producer, promoter, purveyor and prophetess of the famous "Vegetable Compound" which bore her name, and which was doubtless the most widely-known patent medicine in America. There was always glowing testimony to its efficacy, and Mrs. Pinkham herself answered, with no help from secretaries, the thousands of letters seeking advice which came to her from women all over the nation.[2] Long after her death in 1883, her tonic continued to sell, winning a name for its maker in American history (and even a place in a popular song).

In Groton, a small town in Vermont's northeastern corner, Eliza Plumber Welch went into the patent medicine business. Born in the town in 1824, Eliza married Hosea Welch II in 1845 and bore nine children. She began mixing batches of her remedy, which she called "The People's Friend," and selling it to friends and neighbors as a cure for "stomach complaints." Unlike Lydia Pinkham's brew, Eliza's was sold in powdered form, to be mixed with water. Its medicinal value is unknown, but it apparently filled a need, for its manufacture went on for many years (probably out of Eliza's kitchen). In addition to "The People's Friend," Eliza also produced an oint-

ment, which her family always referred to as "Grandmother's salve." It is not known with certainty that Eliza Plumber Welch took her own medicine, but it is known that she lived to be over 100 years of age.

About sixty miles southwest of Groton lies the village of Stockbridge. On the banks of the Tweed River, at a dam built for the purpose, Orson J. Richardson, then twenty-seven years of age and about to be married, purchased a mill complex in 1870 (see page 16). He operated a grist mill, a sawmill and a tub shop, each powered by its own water wheel.[3] When he died in 1878, a month short of his thirty-fifth birthday, there was the question of what to do with the mill. Since his two sons were very young (three years and five months, respectively), it fell to his twenty-seven-year-old widow to take over.

For over ten years Mary Loraine Holmes Richardson ran the mill, an unlikely occupation for a woman of her time. Out of necessity, she had no choice but to get on with it; no Vermonter would shrink from the task. The records are silent about the size of the mill or the number of employees. The fact that Mary Richardson ran the works for a decade suggests that she had more than an average amount of business acumen and a comparable ability as a manager of men.

When she sold the mill, it was to one of her employees, and as late as 1900, the old plant was still sawing lumber. Less than a year after selling the mill, Mary Richardson married again; more of her story is told in "Everywoman — Excerpts from a Diary" (page 81).

In spite of their duties, Eliza Welch and Mary Richardson still made time for their quiltmaking. It would have provided a valuable source of relaxation for these busy women.

1. Ralph Nading Hill, *Yankee Kingdom: Vermont and New Hampshire,* revised edition (New York: Harper & Row, 1973), p. 247.
2. Stewart H. Holbrook, *The Yankee Exodus: An Account of Migration from New England* (Seattle: University of Washington Press, 1968), pp. 330-331.
3. Worth and Mildred Shampeny, "Sawmills in Upper White River Valley, Vermont — 1786 to 1963," *The Northeastern Logger* (April, 1963), p. 18.

"Eliza P. Welch 1852" is carefully but inconspicuously embroidered in tidy white chain stitch in the center of this fine example of whole cloth (or white-on-white) quilting. She wasn't bragging, but she wanted to be sure there was no mistake about who made this quilt; she stenciled her name on the back as well.

Eliza Plumber Welch had good reason to be proud of her quilt. The stitches are tiny and even, fourteen in every inch of quilting. The design is elaborate and well placed, in the finest tradition.

Narrow cords have been drawn between rows of quilting to emphasize the stems and outlines. Its crowning glory, though, is the wide, hand-knotted lace border on three sides. Eliza didn't stop there: she went on to quilt and edge a matching valence for her four-poster bed and a narrow piece which she tacked along the edge of her bedroom shelf.

Whole cloth quilts show off every aspect of a needlewoman's skill. Such quilts were often made as wedding quilts or showpieces: kept for best, put on the bed when important guests were expected, and carefully put away between times. Certainly that is the case with Eliza's quilt, which has survived a century and a half in perfect condition.

Whole cloth, by Eliza Plumber Welch, Groton, 1852, 76 x 78 inches, cottons.
Collection of the May Bonnett family. #3012.

Zeruah Babbitt was true to the times in which she lived when she made this exquisite Rose of Sharon *quilt. The red and green color combination, the lovely symmetry of the appliquéd flower blocks echoed in the quilting pattern between the blocks, the running vine-and-leaf border which turns the corners ever so neatly at the bottom — all are often seen in quilts of the mid-nineteenth century. Zeruah's use of chrome yellow centers and a pink print to complement the solid red of the roses shows her designer's eye; the close quilting covering every inch of the top shows her needlewoman's skill.*

Clearly visible in the quilting at the lower edge of this beautiful piece are two small arms, about the size of a baby's arms, pointing upward with thumbs and first fingers extended. A bracelet is quilted on each tiny wrist. Zeruah was one of the ten children of Polly and Dyer Babbitt. Four of those children perished in a fire in September 1840. Perhaps these tiny arms are a memorial to the brothers and sisters lost just a few years before Zeruah was born.

Zeruah and her younger sister Lutheria made many quilts in their lifetimes, but this one (and Lutheria's companion Princess Feather *opposite) have survived in pristine condition.*

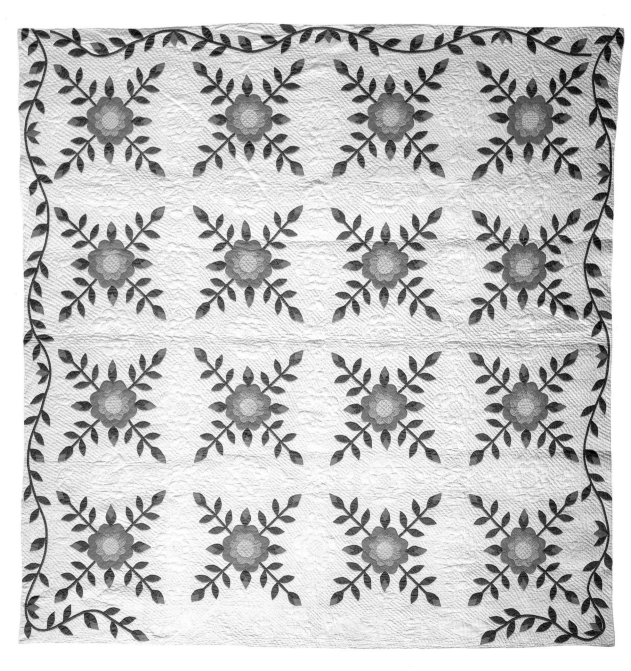

Rose of Sharon, *by Zeruah Babbitt Arnold, Castleton, c. 1860–1870, 83 x 85 inches, appliquéd cottons.*
Private collection, Vermont. #104.

*Lutheria Babbitt quilted with her sister Zeruah. Even without the old family story about the sisters making their quilts together in Civil War times, one would suspect that this fine **Princess Feather** is related to Zeruah Babbitt's **Rose of Sharon** (opposite). One might even think both quilts had been made by the same person: there is the **Rose of Sharon** block in the center, identical to those in Zeruah's quilt; there are also matching fabrics in the two quilts, and some of the quilting designs are similar.*

*Lutheria was a few years younger than Zeruah and, if her quilt is any guide, a bit more exuberant and imaginative. The "feathers" in a **Princess Feather** pattern usually trail gracefully out from the center; Lutheria's have a tight curve at the end, sending the whole design spinning around the central rosebuds.*

Princess Feather, *by Lutheria Babbitt Field Johnson, Castleton, c. 1860–1870, 85 x 79½ inches, appliquéd cottons. Private collection, Vermont. #105.*

Sampler, by Jane A. Blakely Stickle, Shaftsbury, 1863, 80¼ x 80¼ inches, pieced and appliquéd cottons.
Collection of The Bennington Museum. #477.

"In War Time 1863 Pieces 5,602 Jane A. Stickle" reads the embroidered inscription on this quilt, clear evidence of what was on its maker's mind.

There is so much going on in this quilt that one's eye hardly knows where to begin. The 169 blocks are a mix of traditional and original patterns, each rendered in a space four and one-half inches square. The eye is pulled to the border, which resembles so many multi-colored ice cream cones. As if the ice cream cones were not enough, the maker poked, prodded and stretched more pieced patterns to fit the alternating triangles. Even the oddly-shaped corner blocks are given over to patterns. The quilt is a marvel of inspiration, persistence, talent and advanced geometry.

Jane Stickle was fifty when she made this quilt, a woman plainly at the peak of her creative and technical abilities. The fabrics are a sampler, too, a wonderful collection of mid-nineteenth-century textiles, many as crisp and bright as the day they were sewn into the quilt.

A HILL FARM FAMILY

SARAH SMITH WAS BORN IN 1822, GREW UP IN STAFFORD Springs, Connecticut, and came to West Rochester, Vermont, after her marriage to Chester M. Smith. Chester started farming on Rochester West Hill in 1838, when the land was still mostly forest. Over the next twenty years, with Sarah's help, he turned the wooded hillside into a prosperous sheep and dairy farm.

As Sarah's quilt shows, she retained strong ties with her hometown friends and family. Although the one hundred and fifty miles between her old home and her new one was a four day trip in the 1850's, she made that trip at least once, visiting her father in the fall of 1854. Most of what we know about Sarah and her life in Vermont comes from letters she wrote to her husband while she was away.

At that time, Rochester Village was a busy and prosperous community. On the stage route between the college towns of Hanover, New Hampshire, and Middlebury, Vermont, Rochester was home to two general stores, carding and shingle mills, a tannery, a carriage shop, a tailor and milliner, as well as several schools and churches. Even the smaller community of West Rochester had three school districts; the children of the twenty-four families living on West Hill farms were educated at the District #13 school.

Sarah Smith's quilt shows the connections she kept with friends and family after she married and moved to a Vermont hill farm. There are signatures from her birthplace (Westminster, Connecticut), her childhood home (Stafford Springs, Connecticut) and nearby towns (Ashford, Connecticut, and Monson and Springfield, Massachusetts) as well as from her new home in West Rochester.

Sarah's letters to Chester describe a busy round of family visits and the daily chores of a small-town family in the mid-nineteenth century. But it is her plaintive words to her husband as she prepared to come home to the hill farm that clearly portray life on the farm as harder and plainer than life in Connecticut or even in nearby Rochester village: "Chester, I do hope that you will get a stove and table for me by the time that I get home...if you get a stove, get a teakettle and a spider to fit it. I hope you will remember...."

Sarah died ten years after her Connecticut trip, in March 1864, one month short of her forty-second birthday. Less than nine months later, Chester died at the age of forty-four. The inscription on their gravestone reads, "No pains, no griefs, no anxious fear/ Can reach our loved ones sleeping here." The farm they worked so hard to create was eventually abandoned, to be reclaimed by the land. "Today only the foundation stones of his farm buildings and miles of stone walls in the forest give testimony of this once prosperous farm."*

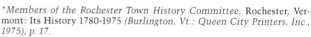

Members of the Rochester Town History Committee, Rochester, Vermont: Its History 1780-1975 (Burlington, Vt.: Queen City Printers, Inc., 1975), p. 17.

Album Patch, *by Sarah M. Smith, West Rochester, c. 1850, 82 x 80 inches, pieced cottons. Collection of Evelyn Billings. #2966.*

Cliora Page spins wool yarn on the steps of the Guindon Farm in Lincoln about 1910, carrying on the longstanding rural tradition of using what was available on the farm to meet the basic needs of the family. Young Lydia Guindon works nearby on her own needlework. Girls in rural areas learned to wield a needle at an early age, and most had mastered sewing techniques by the time they started school.

THE YEARS 1901 TO 1940 begin with the reformation spurred by one Roosevelt of New York and end with the revolution created by another. America went from the dawn of the automobile age to the threshold of the atomic age, from *laissez faire* government by business to New Deal government.

In Teddy Roosevelt the nation had an energetic man who really enjoyed being President, who relished all it entailed, who met the ordinary people of America as easily as he met kings and prime ministers. He flailed away with his "Big Stick" whenever and wherever he thought it necessary, and he promoted reform in many areas where it was badly needed.

Much of this continued under T.R.'s hand-picked successor, William Howard Taft (of Vermont ancestry), and under Taft's successor, Woodrow Wilson. In the twenty years of their presidencies, many basic changes were enacted which affect us to this day—the income tax, pure food and drug laws, limitations on business practices, and railway regulation. Americans fought World War I, the "war to end all wars," but refused to join the League of Nations, preferring instead to disengage and try to achieve their international objectives in other ways.

Lucia Hadley made her quilt sometime before she married Pearl Gaylord in 1890. It is exactly the kind of quilt that an artistically inclined young woman would want to have in her hope chest. Lucia's tulips sway gracefully on curved stems as if gently blown by April breezes. But, lest anyone accuse her of neglecting tradition, she has shown off her needle skills with quilted rosettes between the scattered tulips, on a background of fine diagonal rows of quilting stitches.

Making a scalloped border to fit a four-poster bed must have been a challenge for all of Lucia's skills, and the end result is an interesting cut-out in the corners.

Lucia bequeathed her quilt to her daughter Louise. Louise in turn gave it to her own daughter, a woman as skilled and talented as Lucia herself, who values her grandmother's quilt, she says, "strictly through pride and sentiment."

Tulip *variation, by Lucia Hadley Gaylord, Waitsfield, c. 1880–1890, 92 x 84 inches, appliquéd cottons.*
Collection of Mrs. Charles Tamm. #613.

Family tradition says this quilt was made in 1885 by Alphonose Turcott, from patterns cut by Julian Bellegarde (a fact noteworthy in itself, since the names of non-quilting helpers rarely come down to us). The pink fabric has retained its color, but the other fabric was probably once a fugitive green. Alphonose was no slouch with the needle; the appliqué is precise, the stitches barely visible. At twenty years of age, she was obviously adept at sewing, a skill she would certainly have needed. At the time, Alphonose was housekeeper to her brother, who was Highgate's Roman Catholic priest.

Eleven years later, when her brother was called by his bishop to start a parish at South Hero in Vermont's Lake Champlain Islands, Alphonose went along. It was there that she met and later married Charles Croteau, and where both eventually died.

Appliqué, by Alphonose Turcott Croteau, Highgate, 1885, 72 x 74 inches, appliquéd cottons.
Collection of Suzanne D. Foss. #283.

Mary Ann DaCosta lived with her older sister in Bristol, Rhode Island. Her sister ran a boarding house; her husband was a ship's cook. Once, when he returned from sea, he brought a shipmate; Ansel Sears later married Mary Ann DaCosta. They moved to Irasburg, Vermont, in 1862.

Ansel Sears brought fabrics back from his sea voyages, and Mary Ann used those fabrics to their best advantage. In her later years, Mary Ann lived with her son and taught his five daughters to piece. They remember taking out stitches which were not small or even enough to satisfy grandmother's standards.

Slashed Star *variation, by Mary Ann DaCosta Sears, Irasburg, c. 1880–1890, 80 x 81 inches, pieced cottons.*
Collection of the Sears family. #2703.

On Vermont farms, rows of sunflowers often lend interest to fields of corn, variety to family vegetable gardens, or a splash of color to the house. Because it is the state flower of Kansas, perhaps people think first of that state when sunflowers are mentioned; but, long before the Prairie State was settled, Vermonters grew Helianthus in their yards and fields. Many Vermonters went to Kansas in the 1850's and 1860's, lured by promises of cheap land and rich soil. Limited in what they could take with them, the settlers could have found room for a handful or two of sunflower seeds. Planted shortly after their arrival, the tall, cheerful flowers would have served as a reminder of home.

The signature "Carrie M. Carpenter" on the back of the quilt indicates that she made it prior to her marriage in Northfield in April 1861 to William Smith. No one knows why she used sunflowers as the model for this one-of-a-kind quilt. When her husband died seven years later in an accident, its cheerful colors may have reminded her of happier times. Whatever her motivation and inspiration, she gave posterity a distinctive work of folk art.

Sunflower, by Carrie M. Carpenter Smith Persons, Northfield, c. 1861, 77½ x 84 inches, pieced cottons. Collection of The Shelburne Museum. #511.

This handsome Feathered Star quilt is a striking example of the red and white quilts which were so popular in the closing years of the last century. The combination obviously appealed to at least one of the Ewins sisters of West Berkshire, Vermont, who were born and lived all their lives on the family farm.

This is no design for the faint of heart, no quilt for the beginner. The piecing and appliqué work are both superb, the work of an obviously practiced quiltmaker.

This is one of the few privately-held quilts in the book which is not owned by a descendant of the maker. The owner received it many years ago as a present from her mother, who purchased it from a cousin of the Ewins sisters. Conscious of its meaning to the Ewins family, the owner took it to the same farm where Lovinia and Zenobia lived to show it to their collateral relatives.

Neither sister married. The owner wrote, "My mother always said that the quilt was made by the old maid aunts." If life on the family farm was dull, the sisters knew where to go for entertainment. They made an annual pilgrimage to the horse races at Saratoga, New York, a full day's journey.

Feathered Star, by Lovinia or Zenobia Ewins, West Berkshire, c. 1880–1890, 86 x 86 inches, pieced and appliquéd cottons.
Collection of Prudence Lyon Tomasi. #564.

The dozen years following the war were another matter, and looked back to the nineteenth century rather than forward into the twentieth. The administrations of Harding, Coolidge (another Vermont icon) and Hoover did their best for big business, but let small business, farmers and ordinary Americans shift for themselves.

For some, the Teens and Twenties were a period of prosperity; for others, particularly farmers, the times were hard, a mere warm-up to the Great Depression. It was the age of prohibition, that "noble experiment," of bathtub gin and speakeasies, of religious revivals and loosened morals. It was the age of Sinclair Lewis, H.L. Mencken and Eugene O'Neill, of the Gershwin brothers and Irving Berlin, of Will Rogers, Amelia Earhart and Charles Lindbergh. (At least one Vermonter, Jane Maria Hathorn Brown, commemorated the famous flight in the quilt shown on page 97.) Most of all, it was the age of Henry Ford, for the "Tin Lizzie" and its successors and competitors put America on wheels, gave it a mobility it never had, sent it off in all directions, and eventually maimed American mass transit, the railroads and trolley lines.

The onset of the depression united Americans and much of the world in common misery for a decade. In some of the countries affected by the great global wretchedness, popular dissatisfaction swept governments out of power on waves of violence, but not here. "We owe admiration as well as pity to the simple folk of America who suffered so grievously under the depression. Many by mid-1932 were angry and desperate, but they still had faith in their country and its institutions; surprisingly few listened to strange voices which told them that fascism Mussolini-style, or communism Moscow-style, was the only answer. They were only waiting for a leader to show them the way out."[44]

If change in Vermont from 1900 to 1940 were measured by population, one might conclude that nothing happened: the 1940 population was 359,000, not even 5% more than that of 1900.[45] Vermonters continued to leave the state (always, of course, tell-

ing people elsewhere that it was a fine place to be from). Many were replaced by new people from French Canada, Ireland, Italy and other places. One of the new arrivals, Irene Fortier Betit, was born in Quebec, where there is a tradition of quiltmaking. Her *Feathered Star* quilt (page 91) was made not long after her arrival in this state. The Vermonters who remained re-arranged themselves on the map, as they had been doing since 1840. Maps from 1840, 1880, 1900 and 1980 show a lessening of the fairly even distribution of 1840 to a concentration of population in about two dozen centers in 1880.[46] This trend continued for the next hundred years; today, there are many

towns whose populations are smaller than they were in 1850.

Dairy farming continued to be an important occupation but it was declining in numbers and, like the population, became centered in fewer areas. Manufacturing grew in importance (though the textile industry continued its downhill plunge) and, in some areas such as machine-tooling, Vermont, for a while, led the nation. Exports of items such as marble, granite (and, yes, maple syrup) were important to the state's economy and helped keep alive the non-agricultural side of its reputation.

Like Americans everywhere, Vermonters delighted in the mobility the

automobile provided. As roads improved, it became easier to go to places to which they might not otherwise travel — and they found, sometimes to their dismay, that roads and cars brought a lot of people who never came before. Life as Vermonters lived it for 150 years was on the threshold of a change many of them would greet with mixed emotions. The fifty years to come, especially from 1960 to 1990, would bring profound changes to Vermont's landscape, economy, people and image. For some it would be the best of times, for others the worst, but all would agree that there was no going back to the old Vermont.

Photographed by Grace or Nell Conant, c. 1910–1920 (negative number AQZ 137). From Vermont Album — A Collection of Early Vermont Photographs, ed. Ralph Nading Hill, Copyright ©1974 by The Stephen Greene Press. Used by permission.

George Deering empties a sap bucket into the ox-drawn gathering tank in a Randolph sugar bush. Production of maple syrup and sugar has been an important agricultural activity in Vermont since pioneer days and is still a major source of cash income for many Vermont farms.

Like Sarah Smith, whose quilt is on page 63, Jane Stone lived on a central Vermont hill farm. Less is known of her life; she didn't leave letters or diaries to tell us the details. We do know that Jane and her husband Edwin farmed until late in their lives, when they sold the farm and moved into the town of Randolph. They had two sons: one became a lawyer and settled in Montpelier, the state capital; the other was a farmer in the same Chelsea West Hill area as his parents. Jane's descendants live in central Vermont to this day.

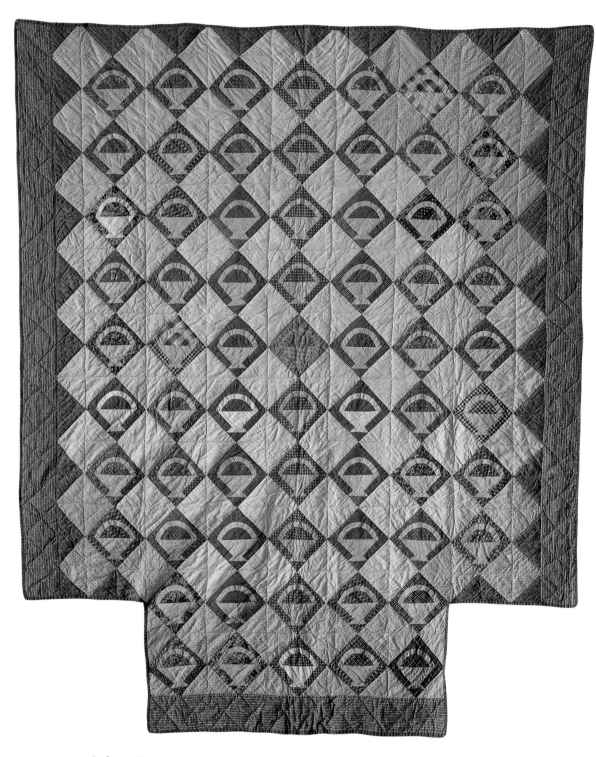

Basket, *probably by Jane Symanthia Ellis Stone, Chelsea, c. 1880, 71 x 85 inches, pieced cottons.
Private collection, Vermont. #2044.*

*This **Ohio Star** is an oddity, with its small (8 x 8½ inches) appliquéd star in the center of a large (40 x 41½ inches) pieced one. The piecing is accurate enough, but the appliqué wobbles a little, and the quilting, although extensive, is simple.*

Born in 1843, Jane lived all her life near Montpelier. Her father, Zenus C. Dewey, had a twin, Julius Y., who went on to become a local physician. Around Montpelier, Dr. Julius Dewey is known as the founder of the National Life Insurance Company, now one of the nation's largest. Jane's cousin George, son of the doctor, achieved a fame of his own when, on May 1, 1898, he sailed into Manila Bay at the head of an American naval squadron. He destroyed the Spanish fleet without the loss of a single American life and came home to a hero's welcome in Vermont, particularly in his hometown of Montpelier, which declared the day of his visit "Dewey Day."

Ohio Star, *by Jane Eliza Dewey Celley, Riverton, c. 1870–1890, 86 x 87½ inches, pieced and appliquéd cottons.*
Collection of Alice Bryant. #33.

AS THE STOCK MARKET collapsed and Wall Street went into a frenzy in October 1929, Vermonters who had no connections to financial institutions or big companies and who owned no stock might have wondered, as country people did everywhere in America, what the fuss was all about. They soon found out; when they did, they didn't much like the news.

Hard times came to the farms and villages of Vermont as surely as to the industrial centers, the cities, and the rural parts of the rest of the nation. Life on the farm, which was never easy, now became even more difficult. Farmers who also held jobs away from the farm stood to lose that employment, while commodity prices dropped lower and lower. Those whose farms were mortgaged, to say nothing of non-farm property owners, faced foreclosure. Tourism declined, manufacturing declined, commerce declined; everything declined except bad news.

Vermonters, who had always found

▷ *Hannah Cressey's quilt is a little like the lives of the Vermonters of her time—plain and orderly, but with spots of color and more than a few sharp edges. Born in 1824, Hannah Cressey lived into the twentieth century. She died in August 1905, just four months after her brother George, with whom she lived on the family farm in South Londonderry, Vermont.*

In most respects, their lives were similar to those of their neighbors and of other country folk in America. Their stern faces and large hands mark them as people who knew hard work, and there is no ostentation in their clothes. In the photo here, she seems to have been caught unawares as the photographer tripped the shutter, for her eyes are closed. Whether or not her eyes were open made no difference; Hannah and George were both blind.

They weren't born blind. Their great-nephew, who was born the year they died and who now treasures her quilt, says that both were victims of an inherited disease, and that they lost their sight in their youth. Long before Hannah made her quilt, she was completely blind. Her great-nephew said other members of the family would cut the pieces and string similar colors together on a thread, then place the strung pieces in Hannah's sewing box. As long as no one meddled with the sewing box, she could distinguish lights from darks and so piece her quilts. And she did *piece: 84 whole blocks, 228 half-blocks, and the whole and half muslin blocks.*

ways to adapt, did so again; they cinched the belts another notch, pared back, cut down, made do. They also continued to vote Republican. No statewide officeholder ever was in real danger of losing his seat. Governors of Vermont might make defiant noises at the new Roosevelt administration, but they turned down very little of the proffered federal assistance. The low-

est point of the Depression was the middle of 1932;[47] assistance was still almost a year away. When help *did* come from the new administration and Congress in Washington, it was broad, deep and swift. The alphabet agencies of the New Deal changed forever the way government did business and touched millions of lives in direct ways previously unknown.

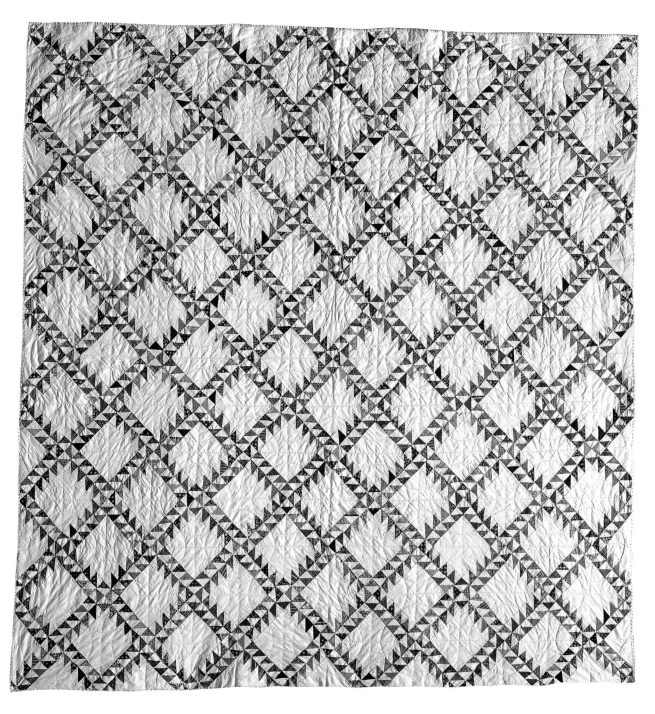

Unnamed pattern, by Hannah M. Cressey, South Londonderry, c. 1870–1890, 77 x 75 inches, pieced cottons. Collection of Mr. and Mrs. Rex C. Doane. #2912.

Embroidered work on a cloth surface has an ancient and honorable history, predating the art of quiltmaking. This striking quilt, with its lavishly decorated blocks, is a particularly good example of the kind of work which, among quilts, is neither fish nor fowl. Its themes hark back to both the crazy quilt (page 48) and the Kate Greenaway (page 82), for many of the blocks carry designs familiar to both kinds of quilts. There are the children and animals so familiar to the (usually) red and white quilts, and the fancy, almost exotic needlework from the crazy quilts.

The colors are bright and cheerful, even on the black background, and some of the designs fairly leap from the surface. Even with all of the black material available to her, Mrs. King still had to piece some of the blocks to make a large enough area for her embroidery. Cynthia Morse Hobbs King was about 60 years of age when she made this fanciful quilt.

Embroidered quilt, by Cynthia Morse Hobbs King, Marshfield, c. 1880–1900, 78 x 78 inches, embroidered wools and cottons.
Collection of Evelyn Stillwell Webler. #2117.

Though most of the federal agencies spent money lavishly in Vermont, the two which probably had the greatest personal impact were the Civilian Conservation Corps and the Civil Works Administration, for both actually put people to work—nationally, over 6.5 million people were employed by the two between 1933 and 1941.[48] Not just in direct employment was the New Deal felt in Vermont; many of the public improvement projects changed the face of the Green Mountain State, with new buildings, roads and reforestation leading the list. For farmers and homeowners, passage of the Emergency Farm Mortgage Act and establishment of the Home Owner's Loan Corporation helped prevent loss of their properties.[49]

Other federal legislation which greatly aided Vermonters was the Soil Conservation Act of 1936 and the creation of the Rural Electrification Agency. This last was of particular importance in sparsely populated Vermont, where private utilities found it unprofitable to extend service to outlying areas. In 1933, it was estimated that no more than 10% of American farms had electricity; by 1941 the number had tripled, and by 1950 about 90% of American farms enjoyed electric power.[50]

For Vermont women, the Depression was one more problem to overcome. It called for all their ingenuity just to live from day to day. Clothes already mended had to be mended again; children's clothes would have to be handed down several times. Larger gardens had to be planted, food stretched further by every means possible, including the extensive use of such things as cornmeal mush. For many Vermont families, credit from the local stores was their salvation, and many local merchants never claimed all their debts.

With the coming of electricity to many hill farms and the eventual start of recovery from the worst of the Depression, some modern and relatively cheap conveniences appeared in Vermont homes. The radio was one of these, and it provided hours of entertainment to its listeners. One envisions a quiltmaker sitting near the radio after the children had gone to bed, scrap basket by her feet, piecing her scrap quilt top by the light of a naked bulb.

Two of our quilts are from the Great Depression, each a popular pattern from that period. The tiny pieces in Frances Slater Rousseau's *Grandmother's Flower Garden* (page 96) are ideal for using up the bits of dresses and blouses left in the scrap basket. Grace Root Wilcox's *Double Wedding Ring* (page 95) would also have utilized scraps for its smaller pieces.

The scrap basket must have been very deep, rich in bits and pieces from the prosperous Twenties or the Gay Nineties, or even from the Centennial period. Cash was in exceedingly short supply, so purchases of new fabrics for clothing would be almost out of the question. Any kind of cotton material would do for the quilt; backing could be made from white commodity bags, and the colored pieces for the tops could come out of the printed cotton feed sacks widely used in the period (the great gift of the feed manufacturers to the quiltmakers of America). The batting might consist of another quilt, too old and worn to be of further use on top of a bed (but *never* so bad that it was to be thrown away), or a blanket in a similar state of decrepitude. In some cases, several worn-out sheets might be put together to fill the need. For quiltmakers, more than ever, it was a time to make do or be forced to do without.[51]

Lady of the Lake, *by M. Helen Bosworth, Bristol, c. 1870–1880, 80 x 86 inches, pieced cottons.*
Private collection, Vermont. #1014.

EVERYWOMAN –
EXCERPTS FROM A DIARY

"The last day of the year of 1900 – Tomorrow will usher in the first day of a new century. A few may see the first of another. Those who have lived in this one have seen wonderful things brought to light and those who live in the one to come will see things even more Wonderful." — diary entry for December 31, 1900

MARY LORAINE HOLMES WAS BORN IN STOCKBRIDGE, Vermont, in 1851. After completing her schooling, she went west, to Palatine, Illinois, to visit relatives. While there she taught school briefly. She was barely sixteen at the time, and returned to Stockbridge one year later. On November 24, 1868, she was certified to teach in the local schools and did so for a short time. Two years later she married Orson J. Richardson, owner of a local mill. Before he died in 1878, they had three children, a daughter who died at the age of two and two sons.

Widowed at twenty-seven, Mary Richardson ran the mill, her home and two children. At the age of thirty-seven she married Frank A. Putnam and started a second family, two daughters and two sons. Like the first-born of her first marriage, the first child of the second was a daughter who also died young. The diaries from the periods of the two deaths, her granddaughter says, record "many days of agonizing as she was aware of the approaching death and then the finality of the death."

Life on the farm in Stockbridge was not easy; diaries from 1891 to 1900 show that she was taking in boarders to augment the farm income. "She writes of whitewashing the ceilings, papering the walls and laying carpet in the chamber and hall," her granddaughter notes. Butter-making was a time-consuming activity, and butter was often used to barter with the neighbors or storekeepers. She tended the hens carefully, for the sale of eggs and dressed chickens meant cash for the household. On December 13, 1891, she wrote, "I was weighed today – 120 pounds." On February 5, 1895, she notes, "I sold Fanny 5# of butter for a $1.00." There are frequently notations about the neighbors helping each other with tasks which might be beyond one family's abilities, such as barn raisings, sheep shearing, butchering, threshing hay or fixing fences. While her family and friends don't sound really poor, there was an obvious lack of cash.

She writes of thimble parties, oyster suppers, medicine shows and meetings of the Ladies Aid Society of the Universalist Church. She talks of sewing clothes and of making quilt blocks for herself or for fundraising quilts for the church. Even on the farm she entertained lots of visitors, who frequently stayed for meals. If the weather was bad, the visitors remained for the night.

On April 21, 1898, there appears the following comment: "War is declared between Spain and the United States." This was of particular concern, for her second son, Jeff, was at Norwich University, the military college in Northfield, Vermont. Four days later, she says, "I had a letter from Jeff – about the War." On May 21, 1898, this appears: "Received a letter from Jeff – he is excited and

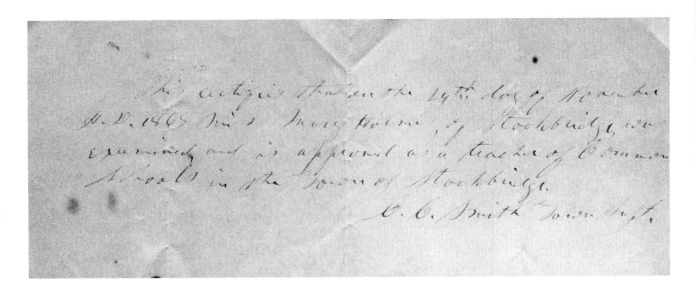

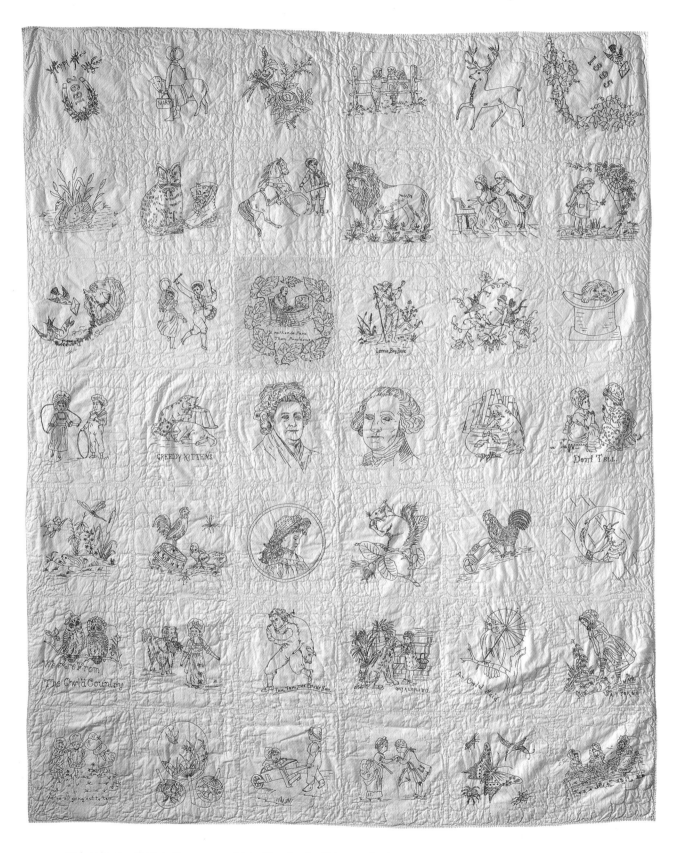

Embroidered quilt (Kate Greenaway style), by Mary Loraine Holmes Richardson Putnam and an unknown quiltmaker, Stockbridge, embroidered 1892–1895, finished after 1930, 68 x 81 inches, embroidered cottons. Collection of Mary Ordway Davis. #2861.

upset about the War." Jeffers Richardson went to Cuba, but he returned safely.

Several entries for 1900 concern themselves with her seven-year-old daughter, Ruth, who had a lame leg, and who was first treated for rheumatism. Here are the entries for December 11 and 12: "Dr. Brigham and Dr. Clough came to examine Ruth's leg. Found it to be infantile paralysis that causes her lameness." "The doctors came to help us use a Galvanic Battery on Ruth's leg and back."

Mary Putnam had the satisfaction of seeing her five surviving children all graduate from high school, no small accomplishment in those days. Besides that, her son Jeff received an engineering degree from Norwich University, and her daughters Ruth and Bernice both graduated from the teacher-training program at the State Normal School in Randolph.

On the day before her seventy-seventh birthday, many members of her family gathered to celebrate. On October 15, 1928, she wrote in her diary, "This is my Birthday—77 years *young* and I thank everyone that remembered me by a token of Love." She died only a few months later, in January, 1929. In her lifetime, she saw the Civil War, electricity, recorded sound, the radio, automobiles and airplanes. She saw the boundaries of the United States stretch to the Pacific Ocean, the acquisition of Alaska and Hawaii, and the adoption of the amendment giving women the right to vote. Hers was a hard life, typical in many respects of those of many nineteenth-century American women. Like them, she bore her lot without complaint and with the stoicism which seems particularly to characterize Vermonters.

◁ *Here is one of those generational quilts which are begun by one quiltmaker and finished by another, perhaps many years later. From the two blocks in the upper corners, we know Mary Loraine Holmes Richardson Putnam began the embroidery in 1892 and finished it in 1895. At the maker's death in 1929, the blocks came into the possession of her daughter. The present owner, granddaughter of the maker, writes, "As a child, I was allowed to very carefully transfer the blocks from one stack to the other as I admired them." Some time later her mother had the blocks set together and the top quilted, though by whom she does not know.*

This type of embroidered quilt was all the rage for a quarter-century, until the 1920's. Based on the designs of the British-born artist and illustrator Kate Greenaway (1846–1901), the blocks usually depict children at play, along with playful animals. Familiar nursery rhymes are depicted, or fairy-tale characters, often with a caption of a very few words. Like their cousins, the crazy quilts, these embroidered pieces gave quiltmakers the opportunity to show off their fancy stitches. Like the crazies, blocks could be purchased.

While patriotic motifs are not uncommon in the Greenaway quilts, it is unusual to find portraits of the first President and his wife. An even greater rarity is the Grover Cleveland block (third row down, third from the left), which depicts the President rocking a cradle, over the words "I'd rather be Papa than President." In his first term (1885-1889), Cleveland wed Frances Folsom in a White House ceremony; in his fifties, the President became a father. Thus we see him in this domestic setting, the proud father rather than the national leader. Cleveland was re-elected in 1892, the year in which these blocks were begun, and served until 1897.

WHEN SECRETARY OF State Thomas Jefferson and Virginia Congressman James Madison stayed at the Dewey House in Bennington in the summer of 1791, they were, they remarked ironically, touring forts and battlefields at the request of President Washington. They were also taking the opportunity, they said innocently, to study the flora and fauna of the region.

This was true, but *barely*, for the men used their northern trip to sound out potential opponents to Secretary of the Treasury Alexander Hamilton. Out of this "botanizing" expedition, as it was called, grew Jefferson's Republican Party, ancestor of today's Democratic Party.

Though Jefferson and Madison were not tourists in the conventional sense, their visit in that first summer of statehood was the precursor of visits by countless people throughout Vermont's history. Some of the visitors liked what they saw so well that they purchased property here and became part-time, sometimes full-time, residents.

Among these were people like Dorothy Thompson and her husband Sinclair Lewis, Norman Rockwell, actor Otis Skinner, Grandma Moses, Robert Frost and composer Carl Ruggles. What they had in common was that each signed his or her name to a quilt block at the Shaftsbury home of another part-time resident, Beatrice Claflin Breese. Mrs. Breese's planting of roots in Vermont came from the simple act of sending her daughter to Bennington College. It was on an early trip to the area with her daughter that Mrs. Breese saw the Shaftsbury property which she pronounced "Simply topping!" She purchased the property, named it the Topping Tavern, and summered there for many years, playing hostess to artists and writers and collecting their signatures on the quilt shown on page 92.[52]

Kansas-born Dorothy Canfield Fisher, a resident of nearby Arlington, was another signer of the Topping Tavern quilt. In 1907 she and her hus-

band, John, took up residence in Arlington. All of her grandparents were Vermonters, and all left Vermont for other states, although her Grandfather Canfield returned to the home place after his retirement. In a house given to her by her great-aunt, Dorothy Canfield Fisher's own children were born (though they, too, eventually left the state), and there she lived and wrote, adding to her already vast store of knowledge about Vermont, its people and its traditions.

It was these observations which led her to write the short play "Tourists Accommodated" in 1932. It recounts the experiences of a Vermont farm family struggling to make enough money to pay the taxes and to send the eldest daughter to teacher's college. The method they hit upon was one then coming into practice in Vermont—taking in summer travelers as paying guests in private homes.

Though the play is cast in a humorous vein, it does delineate the classic conflict between the rural, year-round resident and the seasonal visitor:

"Now take this summer business," the know-it-all tourist says. "If *I* were a Vermonter, I'd build a four-story hotel right down by your waterfalls, and have movies there every night to entertain the guests. City people want to have something to look at when they come to the country. And if *you* had more to look at, you wouldn't be so lonely here winters when everybody goes back to the city."[53]

Vermonters had taken part of that advice over a century earlier and had begun building hotels near the water—not waterfalls, as the tourist suggested, but the many mineral springs which bubbled up through Vermont's landscape. Springs at Clarendon were known as early as 1776; five years later, a log cabin stood at the site to house visitors, to be followed in 1798 by what was probably the first hotel built in Vermont for such a purpose. From Brattleboro in the southeast to Highgate in the northwest, hotels and guesthouses by the dozens sprang up at or near the springs. In their heyday they drew thousands of visitors to Vermont with the promise of miraculous cures for most of the ailments known to humankind. By the 1880's, when there

were at least 131 identifiable spring sites with 32 hotels (some of which had bowling alleys, croquet lawns and bottling works), the spa hotels were on the decline. They went out of business, fell into disrepair and were demolished or burned. Only a handful remain, including the large, handsome brick structure built in 1835 at Clarendon Springs.

Today we scoff at the belief of our ancestors in the extravagant claims of the spring promoters. However, it was more than a matter of health; as Harold Meeks, a University of Vermont geography professor, points out, the springs were "very much a social event. Families and even succeeding generations would return to a resort summer after summer." The mineral

Photograph courtesy of The Bennington Museum.

✳

spring "was considered a home away from home, but rather more elegant." On the positive side, Meeks says, "It was not the mineral water as such that cured ailments and diseases, but rather a change in the diet pattern."[54]

He attributes the demise of the mineral spring business not so much to competition from other regions but to changing preferences. The Vermont landscape, gentler than New Hampshire's, lacking the seacoast of Maine, with fewer diversions than New York, no longer beckoned. The state was seen as "too agricultural, too rural, too familiar for the visitors, many of whom had just stepped off the farm a generation past or even less."[55]

One quiltmaker who benefitted from nineteenth-century tourism was

Bennington has been an important crossroads in southwestern Vermont since the town's founding. Prior to the American Revolution, its Catamount Tavern was a favorite watering spot for Ethan Allen and the Green Mountain Boys. Near the Catamount stood another hostelry, built in 1766 by Elijah Dewey. When General John Stark's New England militia returned victorious from the Battle of Bennington (which was actually fought in New York), the kitchens of the Dewey House provided food for the British, Tory and Hessian prisoners on those August days in 1777. Fourteen years later the Dewey House hosted Secretary of State Thomas Jefferson and Congressman James Madison. Eventually the hotel came to be called the Walloomsac Inn, and stands today, looking very much as it did in this circa 1860 photo.

Lutheria Babbitt Field Johnson of Castleton. Midway between prosperous Rutland and the New York State line, her hometown sat astride the tracks of the Rensselaer and Saratoga Railroad.[56] Hotels at nearby Lake Bomoseen (later home to the writer Alexander Woolcott) hosted many travelers, and it was on the shore of the lake that Mrs. Johnson began taking summer visitors into her home. Her establishment was more like a bed-and-breakfast than a true hotel, but it was one more way for a Vermonter to

A **Log Cabin** design is the perfect vehicle for using up small scraps left over from other projects. In this quilt, the narrow and quite short logs provided the opportunity to empty the scrap basket—or did they?

There are so many repeating fabrics in this quilt that there seem to be only two explanations: That Molona Howe purchased most of the fabric she needed and raided the scrap basket for the rest, or that there were several very large pieces left over, and that these were augmented with other scraps.

This example differs from other **Log Cabin** quilts in its colors. It is more blue than most, and those four pink corners also set it apart. What is so very unlike other **Log Cabin** quilts—almost startlingly so—are the white chimneys. Cut from several different textured, shiny materials (probably shirting fabric), they catch the light and almost give the quilt the appearance of being lit from behind.

The finished top was put away for nearly a half-century; not until 1937 did Molona Howe Blanchard finish the quilt as a wedding present for her nephew and his bride. Mrs. Blanchard was a skilled seamstress who sewed for many families in and around Northfield, Vermont, where she came to live after her marriage. Among her accomplishments were the lace patterns she designed for national magazines in the 1920's and 1930's. The quilt has been lovingly cared for by her niece by marriage, a quiltmaker herself.

Log Cabin, by Molona Howe Blanchard, top pieced, Northfield, c. 1890–1900, backed and tied 1937, 88 x 88 inches, pieced cottons. Private collection, Vermont. #3038.

"Use it up, wear it out, make it do or do without." New Englanders have heard that proverb more times than they care to remember, usually in response to a heartfelt request for something new. This quilt shows that using it up didn't necessarily give a makeshift or unpleasing result.

The pieces in this stunning medallion are tiny, spanning more than fifty years of sewing and saving, from the early 1800's to the 1880's. And, while this quilt was probably not made for "best" (the fabrics are ordinary cottons, the quilting is simple and not particularly fine), there is nothing simple about the design.

Baby Blocks *medallion, unknown maker, Windham County, c. 1880–1890, 89 x 82 inches, pieced cottons. Collection of J. B. Tompkins. #2200.*

wrest a living from the soil. There was a railroad station convenient to the lake, and carriages and coaches ran to hotels around its edge and to other attractions in the area. One could go into Clarendon Springs to sample the famous mineral water there, or to Rutland to shop. Other pursuits consisted of playing croquet on the lawn, strolling along the lakeshore, or simply sitting on Mrs. Johnson's lawn and enjoying the day. When guests retired at night, they might find on their beds quilts of Lutheria's own making—but not, one thinks, the splendid *Princess Feather* on page 59.

It was the perception of Vermont as rural and unspoiled which helped create the next wave of visitors. From the end of World War I to the onset of the Great Depression, automobile tourism in the state boomed, fueled by postwar prosperity, mass-production of relatively cheap cars, and gradual improvements of main highways going through Vermont.

In 1931, the Vermont Commission on Country Life published recommendations for the state's future. One was that tourism ought to be encouraged (though the authors cautioned Vermonters about being too servile on the one hand or too surly on the other), and a second was that vacation-home development should be given a nudge. The Committee evidently felt enough unease at this recommendation to add the following *caveat*: "Where the summer people outnumber the native population, the whole town is occupied in direct contact with them in all capacities from laundress, caddy or waitress to local merchant."

The authors also showed some prescience, warning of the potential for inflated values of agricultural land, thereby making it hard for farmers to survive, and of the problems of seasonal employment. Still, their main thrust was "the extension of the summer homes movement. Everything possible should be done to call the attention of city dwellers to the opportunities that Vermont offers for summer residents." (There was another cautionary note, this one about Manchester, which ten years earlier won praise from an automobile guide as

▷ *There is no doubt whatsoever about the date or maker of this quilt; it proclaims its age and lineage with a prominence unusual in quilts. Emma Marcy Worden was pleased with her work, for her lesson in the geography of Windham County is unique among Vermont quilts. From assorted fabrics, she cut the outlines of the 23 towns, marking each settlement with a red or brown dot and the initials of the village. The town names loop and curve on the map, sometimes bending over backwards to fit the space. Mrs. Worden also labelled the adjacent areas, even the foreign territories of New Hampshire and Massachusetts, and the Connecticut River is a pale blue ribbon which snakes its way along the eastern border.*

Each town was quilted individually on the treadle machine, in diagonal rows laid down a half-inch apart. The towns were then joined together, and the fat, sassy letters were appliquéd by hand. The completed top and backing received enough random machine quilting to hold the layers together.

The Windham County quilt is a wonderful and fanciful (but geographically accurate) piece of work, a folk-art map of Emma Marcy Worden's immediate world. It proclaims the quiltmaker's individuality and imagination.

Emma Worden and her husband Clifton, both natives of Windsor County, Vermont, had one child, a son Harold, who never married; when he became blind in 1969 and entered the Vermont Veterans' Home, he gave the quilt to the neighbors who had cared for him.

being "practically unchanged since the days of the Revolution." The Commission's note said, "In Manchester, particularly, almost all the farms have been turned into summer properties."[57]) For real success, tourism and the summer-home movement needed more of a push than the Commission on Country Life could give it.

In January, 1932, members of the Amateur Ski Club of New York City climbed off their train at the Waterbury station at 4:30 a.m., *en route* to Stowe. They were merely a scouting party for the seekers of wintertime recreation who arrived in ever-growing numbers in the decades to come. The first skiers faced primitive conditions, but with the co-operation and encouragement of state authorities, members of the Civilian Conservation Corps cut trails, built shelters and improved roads leading to the ski areas.[58] The construction of America's first chairlift at Stowe in 1940 spurred the growth of Vermont's ski industry, which remains a major tourist attraction and brings millions of dollars annually into Vermont's economy.

At the end of World War II, the lifting of rationing and the easing of wartime shortages freed Americans to travel for pleasure. Post-war prosperity gave them more disposable income, and better transportation gave them greater mobility. After a decade of depression and five years of war, Americans were ready, willing and able to travel. In the decades following the war, travel and recreation became a greater force in American life. States vied with each other for the tourist business, and it was here that Vermont finally came into its own as all those years of state and private promotional efforts began to pay off.

Americans now knew there was a place called Vermont. For much of the eastern population, the state was within a day's travel. The very qualities about Vermont which contributed to the demise of the mineral spring resorts—its quiet, understated beauty, rural nature and pastoral appearance—now drew people in numbers unimaginable to nineteenth-century Vermonters. Many vacationers became regular visitors; in increasing numbers, some of these acquired property and became full-time residents. This factor, coupled with a large increase in manufacturing and other jobs, led to a dramatic jump in the population. From 1960 to 1990, Vermont gained over 175,000 people, more than the increase in the preceding 150 years. While out-migration continued, the losses were more than offset by new arrivals, and Vermont started writing a new chapter in its history.

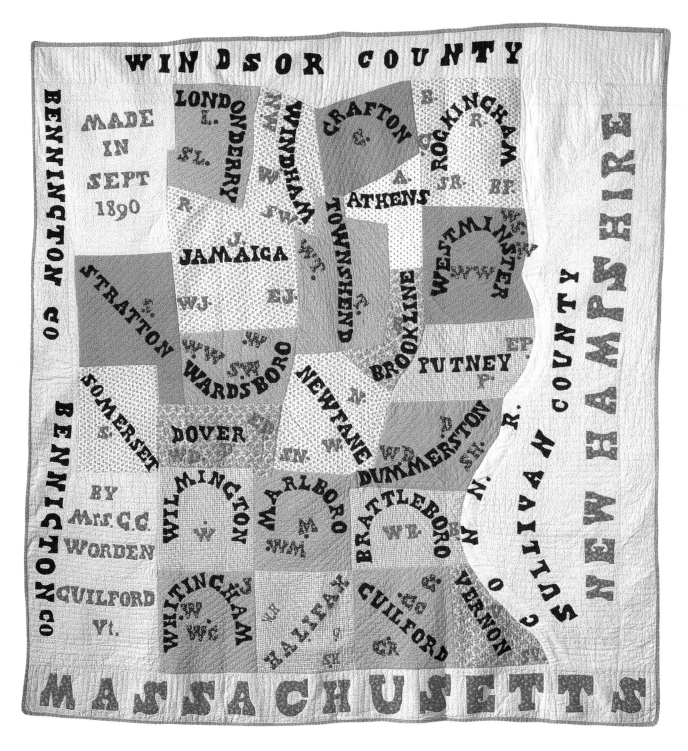

Map of Windham County, Vermont, by Emma Marcy Worden, Guilford, 1890, 80 x 78 inches, pieced and appliquéd cottons.
Collection of Carol and Laurence Lynch, Sr. #3051.

Henry Walker was a Vermont kind of farmer, one who had graduated from Black River Academy in Ludlow, who taught school for a short while before settling down on the farm, who held a variety of town offices and was elected Moderator of Weston Town Meeting. At forty, he married Martha Louise Phillips Dutton; they had children and lived an ordinary farm life.

What is interesting and unusual about Henry Walker is that he was a prolific quilt piecer. As he grew older, he developed arthritis and was eventually bedridden. Having been active all his life, he soon grew tired of lying on his bed with nothing much to do. Someone, perhaps in a fit of exasperation over trying to keep him entertained, gave him a bag of quilt blocks to piece together. He soon became very adept with a needle—a remarkable accomplishment given his arthritis and the fact that some of his fingers had been damaged in a cornshucker accident when he was a small boy.

Soon he was cutting his own pieces; before his death two years later, at the age of 68, he had pieced twenty-one quilt tops. Some of them were finished, but most were not; it was the piecing he enjoyed.

Henry's Double Four Patch is one of those unfinished tops. The fabrics are cottons, and some of them came from the scrapbag of a frugal family member: the top contains fabric from the 1890's as well as the 1920's. There are many colors in this top, and many fabrics, but the cheerful red sashing ties it all together and makes it one that would brighten the days of an invalid.

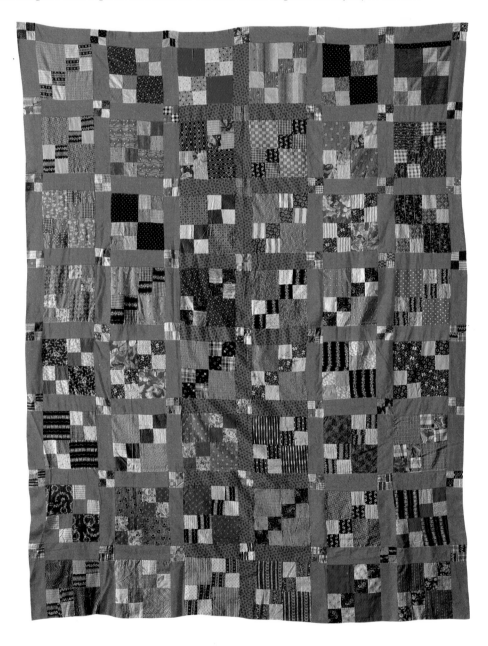

Double Four Patch *top, by Henry Walker, Weston, c. 1920–1927, 72 x 90 inches, pieced cottons. Collection of Kenneth and Anna Walker. #2935.*

Irene Betit, like many other Vermont residents, was born in Quebec. (Canadians, especially those of French origin, have long been the most numerous of Vermont's many immigrant groups.) She was staying in Middlesex, Vermont, when she made this lively Feathered Star *from a Ruby McKim pattern (for which she paid five cents).*

    Ordinarily, the Feathered Star *is a two-color pattern, usually red and white or blue and white, relying on the fanciness of the pattern itself for impact. Not Irene's! She chose the usual red and white, but used a sunshiny yellow as well.*

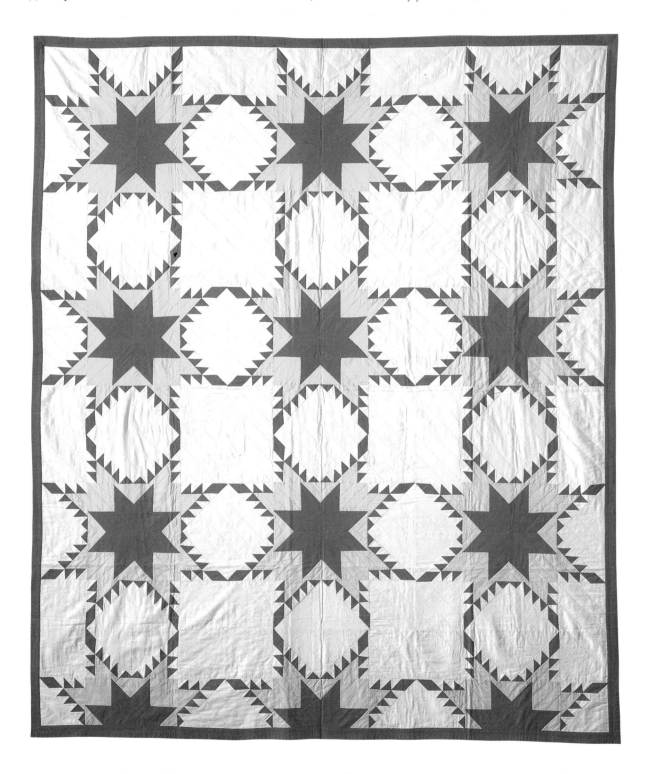

Feathered Star variation, by Irene Fortier Betit, Middlesex, 1932, 77 x 89 inches, pieced cottons.
Collection of Irene Fortier Betit. #2301.

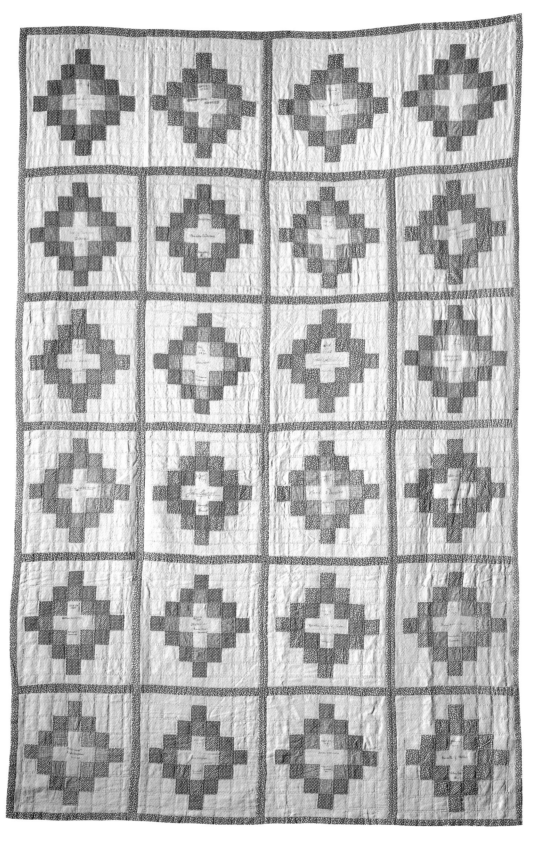

Chimney Sweep, *unknown maker, Bennington County, 1928–1950, 68 x 100 inches, pieced and appliquéd cottons.*
Collection of The Bennington Museum. #484.

The quilt is plain, almost homely, a mix of coarse muslin and the rather garish prints of the 1920's. It is the names on the quilt that attract our attention, for they read like a Who's Who of American arts and letters of the period. There are the writers Sinclair Lewis, Dorothy Thompson, Dorothy Canfield Fisher, Arthur Guiterman, Robert Frost and the Vermont poet and editor Walter Hard. Artists whose names appear are Grandma Moses, Norman Rockwell, Luigi Lucioni and Dean Fausett. There are other kinds of famous people: Otis Skinner, the actor; the composer Carl Ruggles; John H. G. Pell, whose family owned and restored Fort Ticonderoga (site of Ethan Allen's greatest triumph); and Warren R. Austin, first Ambassador to the United Nations and former Vermont Senator. John Spargo, historian of Bennington, Vermont, added his name, as did Sarah Cleghorn, the Socialist, pacifist and anti-vivisectionist, perhaps best known for the lines "The golf links lie so near the mill/That almost every day/The laboring children can look out/And see the men at play."

The names were collected between 1928 and 1950 by a woman who played host to these and other prominent artists and writers at her home in Shaftsbury, Vermont. Beatrice Claflin Breese came from a well-to-do New York family, and first saw the house, built in Vermont's independence year of 1777, when her daughter was at Bennington College. Liking what she saw, Mrs. Breese purchased the property from a descendant of the builder and christened it the Topping Tavern (so-called because, upon first seeing it, she pronounced it "Simply topping!").

Two years after purchasing the tavern, Mrs. Breese divorced her husband and married an Englishman, Archibald Charles Montagu Brabazon, fifth Earl of Gosford, a recent immigrant to America. Lord Gosford died in 1954, and his wife in 1967. On her death, the property was bequeathed to the Bennington Museum, which operated it for some years as the Topping Tavern, and later as the Peter Matteson Tavern (for the builder).

There is no indication as to the name of the maker of the quilt; perhaps her interest in the Americana with which she filled the tavern inspired Lady Gosford to make the quilt herself. As simple as it is, it was more than suitable as a vehicle for the signatures of some of the famous people who have spiced the life of Vermont.*

*Letter from Ruth Levin, Registrar, The Bennington Museum, April 1990.

In 1921 or 1922, Mattie Atwell Waite, then over ninety years of age, paid an extended visit to her niece, Rosalie Beecher Macomber (then a sprightly 56 or so) in Johnson, Vermont. During the visit, the two women tied or quilted a number of quilt tops, some of which were pieced at about the same time.

Mattie Atwell Waite made more than fifty quilts during World War I, reports her great-niece, owner of the quilt. She was then living in the Lowell, Massachusetts, area where, like so many other young Vermont women, she went to work in the mills. Many of the pieces in this and the other quilts she made would have come from those same mills.

What you see here is really only part of the story of this quilt, for you are looking at one side; the other is a **Spider Web** (called "Joseph's Coat" by the family). The sampler, the owner says, was made from left-over blocks of the quilts her mother and great-aunt finished during their marathon. (Some blocks, of much earlier fabrics, must surely have been in the sewing or scrap basket for a number of years.) Lacking enough of any individual pattern to make a whole quilt, and yet unable to throw away the remnants, the two women did what any self-respecting Vermonter brought up on the doctrine of frugality would do: they put them into a quilt.

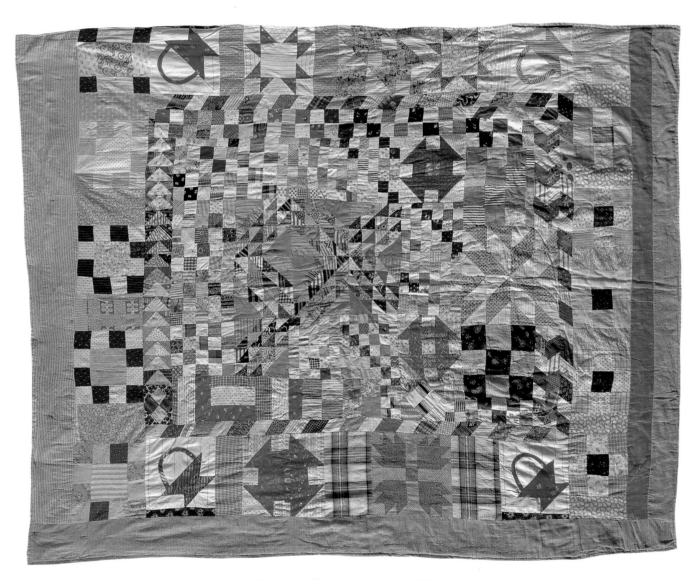

Sampler, by Rosalie Beecher Macomber and Mattie Atwell Waite, Johnson, 1921–1922, 63 x 80 inches, pieced and appliquéd cottons.
Collection of Bernice Cameron and family. #2571.

The Double Wedding Ring *is another of the very common patterns which lead a casual observer to say, half aloud, "Oh, yes, a typical thirties quilt," and pass along without looking at it too closely. This wedding ring, however, is anything but typical. Using only the fabrics common in the early thirties, Grace Root Wilcox set the bands, pieced from bits of pastel floral fabrics, against solid green and pink backgrounds, where a quiltmaker with less vision and daring would have used white.*

Grace made many quilts for her family in the 92 years of her life, some of them quilted with other members of the women's group at the first Congregational Church in Manchester, Vermont. Her husband Burton often helped her with the quilting frame and, according to the family, "was always around to help if she had any problems in her designs." Grace was an active member of the Equinox Grange in Manchester, too, as might be expected of a modern farm woman in the early twentieth century. But her interests went beyond family, farm and church. Grace was a young woman during World War I. When the second war came, she joined the Aviation Observers Corps and worked as a vehicle operator for the American Red Cross in nearby Bennington.

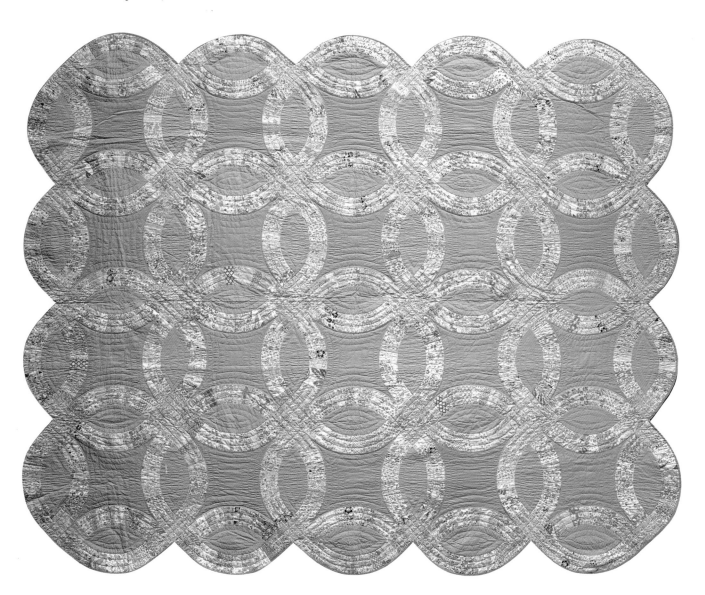

Double Wedding Ring, *by Grace Root Wilcox, Rupert, c. 1930, 77 x 96 inches, pieced cottons.*
Collection of Bernie and Phyllis Wilcox. #2304.

Grandmother's Flower Garden *quilts ranked as one of the most popular patterns of the twentieth century, especially from the 1920's on. Perhaps because there are so many, a viewer may become jaded, and one's eye may slide past one without really taking it in. This quilt demands attention, though; the placement of the colors and the subdued green of the paths and borders, when combined with heavy and exquisite quilting, give this a special quality. Even the squared-off edges set this apart from most others, which tend to carry their hexagons right out to a scalloped (and sometimes scraggly) edge.*

Early in the Great Depression, Frances Rousseau offered to make a quilt for a neighbor, for whom she had been doing dress alterations, at the rate of ten cents per hour (not a very large salary, even in the Depression — but, historically, quiltmakers have not commanded large salaries). When the quilt was completed, the neighbor, Mrs. Arthur Dunton Perry, paid Mrs. Rousseau the sum of one hundred dollars — and that was a goodly price for a quilt in the cash-poor thirties. No one looking at the quilt today would dispute the fact that it has a thousand hours' work in it.

Lovingly cared for by Mrs. Perry's niece, the quilt is a superb example of a common pattern made uncommon by a woman with a keen eye for color and a skilled hand with a needle.

Grandmother's Flower Garden, *by Frances Slater Rousseau, Barnard, c. 1930–1935, 80 x 90 inches, pieced cottons.*
Private collection, Vermont. #137.

Even today, more than sixty years after his history-making trans-Atlantic flight, the name of Charles Lindbergh brings to mind adventure, daring and the thrill of being first. In the thirties, Lindbergh was a genuine folk hero. Every boy and many a girl longed to be an aviator.

When Lindbergh landed at Hartness Airport in Springfield, Vermont, on July 26, 1927, he was greeted by a crowd 30,000 strong. It was quite a gathering, ten percent of the entire population of the state at the time!*

Times were hard in Vermont in the thirties. When Jane Hathorn Brown made this quilt, she used the materials at hand to piece the planes. And, following another good Vermont tradition, she used another quilt, already worn with long use, as the filler. The quilting is simple; with the extra layers of a completed quilt inside, it would have been difficult to make many tiny stitches. But we can tell that the design was at least partly inspired by Lindbergh's historic flight, for quilted in the large plain blocks between the planes are the heads of eagles. "Lucky Lindy" was also known as "The Lone Eagle."

Jane Brown's son remembers helping his mother with her quilting, and he still treasures his **Airplane** quilt, even though it is now tattered and worn.

*Charles Edward Crane, Let Me Show You Vermont *(New York: Alfred A. Knopf, 1942), p. 310.*

Airplane *(detail), by Jane Maria Hathorn Brown, Bethel, c. 1930, 76 x 78 inches, pieced cottons.*
Collection of Thelbert D. Brown. #3009.

T HE TWIN CURRENTS OF Vermont and American history are inextricably intertwined. Often Vermonters were in the forefront of national events, such as westward migration and the promotion of universal education, as illustrated respectively by the Palmer quilt (page 45) and the Randolph friendship quilt top (page 55). During the Civil War, Vermonters responded to the needs of the nation with an enormous outpouring of volunteers for the preservation of the Union and of money and material goods for the support of those troops. Jane Stickle's quilt (page 60) shows that the thoughts of those at home were with the men at war. In the 1890's, Emma Worden and Cecile Depoutee took note of Vermont and American geography (pages 89 and 48). In this century, Jane Brown commemorated Lindbergh's trans-Atlantic flight (page 97), and Grace Wilcox and Frances Rousseau showed in their quilts (pages 95 and 96) the effects of the Great Depression.

Neither those who left the state nor those who remained could entirely escape their heritage: the self-reliance, industry, thrift and integrity for which Vermonters are known. These qualities are evident in many of the quilts presented here, such as the original designs used in the Carpenter *Sunflower* (page 68) and the Bolster *Peony* (page 35); quilts which have thousands of pieces like the *Baby Blocks* medallion (page 87) and the *Log Cabin* (page 86); and scrap quilts like the Rich *Nine Patch* variation (page 32) and the Macomber/Waite sampler (page 94). The quilts made by Hannah Cressey (page 75) and Henry Walker (page 90), which show the makers' desires to contribute to family life in spite of their handicaps, emphasize these traits.

In the face of a tidal wave of change, Vermonters have clung to their heritage as a rock of salvation. The same qualities which appear in the quilts mentioned above sustained Vermonters whether they were setting up schools in the midwest, breaking the sod of western prairies, mining gold in California or eking out a living on the farm in Vermont.

Whether women made quilts of their own design or followed patterns popular in other parts of the country, they always used their quilts for more than simple bedcoverings. Quiltmaking afforded a reason to get together with other women and a way to remember distant friends. It provided one of the few avenues of artistic expression open to women in an age when women's art, the art of the home, was not considered significant. It was also a way to attain what contemporary Massachusetts quiltmaker Nancy Halpern calls "the desire to leave something behind." People around the world who are looking for new ways to explore the past and deal with the present have endowed quilts with a significance unforeseen by quiltmakers of preceding generations. This new historical perspective and artistic appreciation confers immortality upon the quilts and their makers. The quilts of Vermont, like those of the nation, are the makers' way of saying to their descendants, and to the world at large, "Here is a token of myself and of my life. Care for it well."

Members of the Thimble Club pose around the quilt frame on the north lawn of the Pierce family home in North Shrewsbury about 1930. Gertrude Pierce (second from right) and her daughter Marion (second from left) were among the members of this sewing and social group which met at the homes of its members or at the then vacant North Shrewsbury parsonage. Club members made quilts which they donated or raffled for the benefit of local organizations.

FOOTNOTES

1. Frederic F. VandeWater, *The Reluctant Republic: Vermont, 1724-1791* (Taftsville, Vt.: The Countryman Press, 1974), p. xv.

2. Workers of the Federal Writers' Project of the Works Progress Administration for the State of Vermont, *Vermont: A Guide to the Green Mountain State* (Boston: Houghton Mifflin Company, 1937), p. 29.

3. VandeWater, p. xix.

4. Dorothy Canfield Fisher, *Vermont Tradition* (Boston: Little, Brown and Company, 1953), pp. 163-167, 183.

5. Ruth Levin, "Dress Uniform, 1803," in *Highlights from the Bennington Museum* (Bennington, Vt.: Bennington Museum, 1989), p. 59.

6. Ralph Nading Hill, *Yankee Kingdom: Vermont and New Hampshire*, revised edition (New York: Harper & Row, 1973), p. 161.

7. Charles T. Morrissey, *Vermont: A History* (New York: W. W. Norton & Company, 1984), pp. 111-112.

8. Charles Edward Crane, *Let Me Show You Vermont* (New York: Alfred A. Knopf, 1942), p. 145.

9. Morrissey, p. 112.

10. Daniel J. Boorstin, *The Americans—The National Experience* (New York: Random House, 1965), p. 144. Quoted in Louise B. Roomet, "Vermont as a Resort Area in the Nineteenth Century," *Vermont History*, XLIV, no. 1 (Winter 1976), 4.

11. Morrissey, p. 109.

12. Linda Otto Lipsett, *Remember Me: Women & Their Friendship Quilts* (San Francisco: The Quilt Digest Press, 1985), pp. 16-20.

13. Lipsett, p. 16.

14. Lipsett, pp. 19-20.

15. Virginia Gunn, "Quilts for Union Soldiers in the Civil War," in *Uncoverings 1985*, ed. Sally Garoutte (Mill Valley, Calif.: American Quilt Study Group, 1986), p. 114.

16. Fisher, pp. 232-233.

17. Fisher, pp. 229-230; Edmund Fuller, *Vermont: A History of the Green Mountain State* (Brattleboro, Vt.: The Vermont Printing Company, 1952), p. 161.

18. Fuller, p. 162.

19. Fisher, p. 232.

20. Fisher, p. 254.

21. Fisher, pp. 233-237.

22. G. G. Benedict, *Vermont in the Civil War*, I (Burlington, Vt.: The Free Press Association, 1886), pp. 23, 34-36.

23. Fuller, p. 165.

24. Morrissey, p. 34.

25. Fisher, pp. 240-241.

26. Harold A. Meeks, *Time and Change in Vermont: A Human Geography* (Chester, Conn.: The Globe Pequot Press, 1986), p. 198.

27. Morrissey, p. 123.

28. Meeks, pp. 104, 177.

29. Walter B. Gates, "Native Vermonters in Other States," *The Vermonter: A State Magazine*, VII, no. 7 (Feb. 1902), 54-55.

30. Meeks, p. 87.

31. H. N. Muller, III, letter to Richard L. Cleveland dated August 24, 1990.

32. Stewart H. Holbrook, *The Yankee Exodus: An Account of Migration from New England* (Seattle: University of Washington Press, 1968) pp. 211-212, 219-220.

33. Holbrook, p. 322; Samuel Eliot Morison, *The Oxford History of the American People* (New York: Oxford University Press, 1965), pp. 729, 732.

34. Holbrook, pp. 341-343.

35. Morrissey, p. 114.

36. Morrissey, p. 21.

37. Morrissey, p. 160; Crane, p. 202.

38. Holbrook, pp. 38, 170, 173, 79-80.

39. Holbrook, pp. 39-45.

40. Holbrook, pp. 305, 85.

41. Holbrook, p. 305.

42. Holbrook, p. 298.

43. Crane, p. 201.

44. Morison, p. 947.

45. Meeks, p. 177.

46. Meeks, pp. 182-183, 215-216.

47. Morison, p. 944.

48. Morison, pp. 955-956.

49. Morison, p. 958.

50. Morison, p. 965.

51. The Vermont Quiltsearch documented a number of quilts from the Depression period which used worn-out quilts or blankets in lieu of batting. One quiltmaker in her seventies described how she helped her mother make a quilt which used worn sheets for a filler. Both printed and white feedsack material showed up regularly in quilts from this period.

52. Ruth Levin, letter to Richard L. Cleveland dated April 30, 1990.

53. Dorothy Canfield Fisher, *Tourists Accommodated* (New York: Harcourt, Brace and Company, 1932), pp. 64-65.

54. Meeks, p. 153.

55. Meeks, p. 155.

56. Meeks, pp. 108, 116.

57. Meeks, pp. 221, 227-229.

58. Meeks, p. 233.

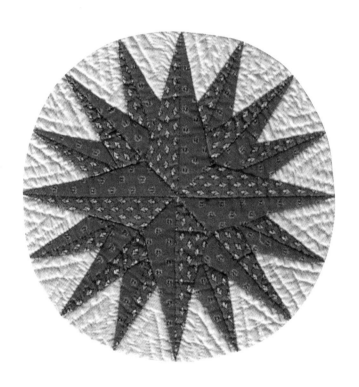

AFTERWORD

Only in recent years has the general public come to regard quilts as anything other than bedcovers. A quilt is also a testimony to its maker — to her vision, her artistry and her skill. In their quilts, Vermonters left behind a record of life in their home state. The Vermont Quiltsearch is an attempt to locate and identify quilts before they deteriorate with age and lose their oral history.

Plain and Fancy and the companion touring show are results of the Quiltsearch, a project of the Vermont Quilt Festival. Timed to coincide with the 1991 bicentennial of Vermont statehood, Quiltsearch staff and community volunteers conducted a county-by-county search for quilts made in Vermont from pioneer times until 1941. Focusing on family quilts and quilts in private collections, the Quiltsearch photographed and established written records for more than 1100 quilts at twenty documentation sites. Records of 2000 quilts documented by the Vermont Quilt Festival between 1979 and 1989 yielded another 800 Vermont-made quilts.

From all these records, we chose the forty-five quilts presented to you here. We based our selections on the quilts themselves, the willingness of quilt owners to participate in the project (which involved innumerable phone calls, letters and visits in addition to entrusting their family treasures to the Quiltsearch) and the availability of information about the quilts and quiltmakers.

To our sorrow, we found that we were a generation too late to capture the stories of many quilts. While quilt owners, many in their seventies and eighties, welcomed our interest and freely shared the information they had, their parents and grandparents were the last to know the secrets and significance of the quilts they handed down to the next generation.

The Quiltsearch Committee and the Vermont Quilt Festival continue to be vitally interested in quilts made in Vermont prior to 1960. Anyone owning or knowing of such quilts is invited to write to us at:

Vermont Quiltsearch
P.O. Box 349
Northfield, Vermont 05663

All replies are treated as confidential.

QUILTS IN VERMONT MUSEUMS
AND HISTORICAL SOCIETIES

The following Vermont museums and historical societies provided information to the Vermont Quiltsearch. It is advisable to call ahead of time to check on the public hours or to make arrangements to see the quilts.

Barre Museum
Verbena Pastor, Curator
Aldrich Public Library
P. O. Box 453
Barre, Vt. 05641
(802) 479-1801

19 quilts; 3 usually on display; no admission charge. Miscellaneous textile products and related items.

The Bennington Museum
Ruth Levin, Registrar
West Main Street
Bennington, Vt. 05201
(802) 447-1571

50 quilts; number on display varies; admission charge. Miscellaneous textile products and related items.

Billings Farm and Museum
Robert Benz, Curator
P. O. Box 489
Woodstock, Vt. 05091
(802) 457-2355

75 quilts in storage may be seen only by appointment; museum open May 1 to end of October; admission charge. 19th-century clothing and domestic publications; some textile implements.

Brookfield Historical Society
Debbie McAskill
RFD
Brookfield, Vt. 05036
(802) 276-3394 or call
Town Clerk at (802) 276-3352

8 quilts, 5 usually on display; donations accepted. Miscellaneous textile products and sewing implements.

Chester Historical Society
Donna Ohl Allen
Flamstead Road
Chester, Vt. 05143
(802) 875-2016

14 quilts; 6 to 8 usually on display; donations accepted. Some Victorian and 1920's costumes.

Community Historical Museum of Mt. Holly
Janice Bamforth
P.O. Box 26
Belmont, Vt. 05730
(802) 259-2283

9 quilts on display; donations accepted. Miscellaneous costumes, 1850-1930.

Concord Historical Society and Museum
Bernice Payeur
HCR 60, Box 40
North Concord, Vt. 05858
(802) 695-2288

7 quilts on display; donations accepted. Miscellaneous costumes, 1880-1920.

The Fairbanks Museum and Planetarium
Ruth Crane or Kathy Armstrong
Main and Prospect Streets
St. Johnsbury, Vt. 05819
(802) 748-2372

7 quilts; may be seen by appointment; admission charge. Miscellaneous textile products and related items.

Highgate Historical Society
Evangeline Malaney
P. O. Box 71
Highgate Center, Vt. 05459
(802) 868-4984

4 to 6 quilts; may be seen by appointment; donations accepted.

Historical Society of Windham County
Alice Williams
P. O. Box 32
Newfane, Vt. 05345
(802) 365-4409

10 quilts; may be seen by appointment; donations accepted. Miscellaneous textile products.

Londonderry Historical Society and Museum
Patricia W. Wiley
RR 1, Box 41
South Londonderry, Vt. 05155
(802) 824-5268

2 quilts on display; donations accepted.

Moretown Historical Society
Evelyn Goss
Moretown, Vt. 05660
(802) 496-3601

3 quilts; all on display; donations accepted.

Noyes House Museum
Morristown Historical Society
Dawn Andrews, Curator
Sand Hill
Morrisville, Vt. 05661
(802) 888-5605; summers: 888-7617

14 quilts; 2 usually on display; donations accepted. Linen, wool and linsey-woolsey textiles, hooked rugs and clothing (1840-1920); miscellaneous implements.

Old Constitution House
Windsor, Vt. 05089

Some quilts on display; others in storage; admission charge. To view collection, call William W. Jenney at (802) 672-3773.

Orleans County Historical Society, Inc.
Old Stone House Museum
Reed Cherington, Museum Director
RFD#1 Box 500
Orleans, Vt. 05860
(802) 754-2022

20 quilts; 2 usually on display; admission charge. Approximately 1,000 costume and textile items and related artifacts.

Plymouth Notch Historic District
Calvin Coolidge Birthplace
William W. Jenney
P. O. Box 79
Plymouth, Vt. 05056
(802) 672-3773

15 to 20 quilts; some on display; admission charge. Coolidge family memorabilia includes quilt made by Calvin Coolidge at age ten.

Randolph Historical Society, Inc.
Wes Herwig, Curator
P. O. Box 15
Randolph Center, Vt. 05061
(802) 728-5398

10 to 12 quilts; 2 to 3 on display; admission charge. Miscellaneous textile products.

Rochester Historical Society
Edith Artz
Leister Road
Rochester, Vt. 05767
(802) 767-4440

4 quilts; 2 on display; donations accepted. Miscellaneous textile products and related items.

Rutland Historical Society
Eleanor Elwert
19 Crescent Street
Rutland, Vt. 05701
(802) 773-3417

5 quilts in collection may be seen by appointment. Some handwork and costumes.

St. Albans Historical Museum
Anna M. Neville
P. O. Box 722
St. Albans, Vt. 05478
(802) 527-7933

25 or more quilts; 7 to 8 on display; admission charge. Fisk loom sample book; miscellaneous textile products and related items.

Saxtons River Historical Society
John H. Lucy
Box 546
Saxtons River, Vt. 05154
(802) 869-2657

5 quilts; all on display; donations accepted.

Shelburne Museum
Celia Y. Oliver, Curator
Rt. 7
Shelburne, Vt. 05482
(802) 985-3346

400+ quilts in collection; 100+ on display; admission charge. Sample books with printed fabrics; numerous household accessories; sewing machines, tools and manuals. Museum open mid-May to mid-October; research facilities open year-round by appointment.

The Sheldon Museum
Ginna Brown or Peggy Lyons
1 Park Street
Middlebury, Vt. 05753
(802) 388-2117

3 quilts in collection; admission charge. Miscellaneous textile products and sewing implements.

Vermont Historical Society
Mary Labate Rogstad, Registrar
109 State Street
Montpelier, Vt. 05602
(802) 828-2291

70 quilts; 1 or 2 on display; donations accepted. Sample books, miscellaneous textile products and related items.

Westminster Historical Society Museum
Karen Larsen, Curator
Rt. 5
Westminster, Vt. 05158
(802) 722-4203

1 quilt on display; donations accepted. Miscellaneous textile products and related items.

Williamstown Historical Society
Janice M. MacAskill, Curator
Route 1 — Box 612
Williamstown, Vt. 05679
(802) 433-5475

1 quilt displayed occasionally; donations accepted. Miscellaneous textile products and related items.

Winooski Historical Society
Mary E. Fitzgerald
21 Park St.
Winooski, Vt. 05404
(802) 863-6471 or 655-3561

No quilts; donations accepted. Miscellaneous textile products and related items; samples from several local woolen mills.

Woodstock Historical Society
Gregory C. Schwarz
26 Elm Street
Woodstock, Vt. 05091
(802) 457-1822

14 quilts; 3 to 4 on display; donations accepted. Miscellaneous textile products and related items.

Simply the Best

THE QUILT DIGEST PRESS

Dept. D
P.O. Box 1331
Gualala, CA 95445